D1356131

HOW TO DRESS SALMON FLIES

HOW TO DRESS
SALMON FLIES

A Handbook for Amateurs

T. E. Pryce-Tannatt

With an Appreciation by T. Donald Overfield
Additional material compiled by
John Veniard and Freddie Riley
Drawings by Donald Downs

A & C Black
London

Part One first published 1914
Second edition (Parts One and Two) 1977
Reprinted 1986
A & C Black (Publishers) Ltd
35 Bedford Row, London WC1R 4JH

Part One © 1914 T. E. Pryce-Tannatt
Part Two © 1977 John Veniard
Drawings in Part Two © 1977 Donald Downs

ISBN 0-7136-1618-0

Text printed in Great Britain by
Hollen St Press Ltd, Slough, Berkshire.
Colour plates printed by White Quill Press,
Mitcham, Surrey

CONTENTS

PART TWO

COLOUR PLATES

In Plates XIII-XVI Adjutant, Black Joke, Blue Joke,
Candlelight, Embers, Wrack were tied by Terry Griffiths;
the remainder were tied by Freddie Riley.

PRYCE-TANNATT: AN APPRECIATION

BY T. DONALD OVERFIELD

The period covered by the latter years of the nineteenth century and the early part of the twentieth could rightly be called the "Flamboyant Era" of salmon fly design and dressing, for the jewel-like beauty of the Victorian patterns have never been equalled.

The student of salmon fly design can, at this distance in time, tend to ignore the vexing question of the salmon taking abilities of such creations, compared to modern patterns sporting hair-wings and displaying a general paucity of feathers, concentrating instead upon the techniques devised by the great fly tyers of the period in question.

Three major books on salmon fly dressing emerge from that era: "How to Tie Salmon Flies" by Capt. J. H. Hale, published in 1892; "The Salmon Fly: How to Dress It and How to Use It" by George M. Kelson, published 1895 and "How to Dress Salmon Flies" by Pryce-Tannatt, published 1914. For lucidity and practicality the latter volume has yet to be bettered, despite the passage of almost sixty years.

Just who was the author, for despite the undoubted popularity of his classic work he was to write but one further book, lightweight in comparison, entitled "Meditations of a Middle Aged Angler", written during the years of the second world war.

Dr. Thomas Edwin Pryce-Tannatt, O.B.E., M.B., B.S., D.P.H.(ENG) was born in the year of 1881 in the East Indies, though his family were of Montgomeryshire extraction. At the appropriate age he returned to the United Kingdom to take up his education, attending Shrewsbury school and passing on to University College Hospital. His interest in salmon fishing and the ecology of the rivers caused him to forsake medicine and in the autumn of 1912 he accepted the appointment of Inspector of Salmon Fisheries in the Board of Agriculture and Fisheries. Early in the same year he had taken over as editor of the Salmon

and Trout Association magazine, following
in the footsteps of J. B. Fielding and
H. T. Sheringham, though upon taking office
with the ministry he gave up the editorship.

Any man who can combine his sporting
interests with his profession is indeed fortunate and Pryce-Tannatt approached his new
appointment with enthusiasm. His effect was
soon to be noticed in the oft-time slow
corridors of the Civil Service, doing notable
work not only in the interests of the sporting
salmon angler but with the genuine interest
of the salmon fishing industries always in
mind. That he managed to maintain a
balanced outlook between the sometime
warring factions says much for the fairness of
the man. During his years of office, from 1912
until 1946, Pryce-Tannatt achieved a great
deal, though he is possibly best remembered
for the Salmon and Freshwater Fisheries
Act of 1923 and the reorganisation of the
various river-board authorities. His efforts
in the designing and construction of fish
passes brought him recognition, the results
of his work in this direction being contained
in a series of lectures, the "Buckland Lec-

tures", published as a paper in 1937 under the title of "Fish Passes".

His work of thirty-four years ended in 1946 when he retired at the age of sixty-five. Now he was free to once more fully indulge his passion for salmon fishing, a welcome guest on so many ideal salmon rivers throughout the country, rivers that he had done so much to improve and maintain. His declining years were spent in his home county of Montgomeryshire, close by the river Dovey.

Towards the end of his life ill-health forced him to hang up his rods, however, the beautifully laid out gardens at his home testified to his secondary interest. He died on April 19th, 1965 at the good age of eighty-four.

Pryce-Tannatt lived to see a second edition of "How to Dress Salmon Flies" published in 1948, by A. & C. Black the original publishers, and a new generation of fly tyers were able to benefit from his clear practical instruction into the complex craft of tying the traditional turn of the century salmon patterns.

And now, the third edition is with us. Many of the feathers, once so commonplace in the days when Pryce-Tannatt wrote the original volume, are now no more, and we must look for substitutes. Such substitution is possible, as one will see from the additional material within this third edition. No-one would read these new pages with a more lively interest, and I would judge, approbation, than the original author.

Pryce-Tannatt's approach to fly dressing can best be determined from a passage found on page two of the first edition:

> ". . . there is an indescribable something about a fly dressed by an expert amateur, who is a practical salmon fisherman, which the fly dressed by a non-angling professional not infrequently lacks. I have heard this peculiar quality rather neatly referred to as 'soul'. A precise explanation of what is meant by 'soul' is one of the impossibilities. The term is incomprehensible to the uninitiated, but is completely understood by the experienced man".

There lies the spirit of the man.

T. Donald Overfield,
Solihull,
Warwickshire.

PREFACE

IT will be admitted generally that for the purpose of learning the art of dressing flies one hour's practical demonstration by an expert will be of more service than whole volumes of written directions. Nevertheless, the latter are, I think, of some use, and will at least serve the purpose of permanently recording certain points of manipulation to which attention may have been drawn in a practical demonstration and which are apt to escape the memory.

Verbal precept, backed up though it may be by ocular demonstration, will, by itself, be of no more permanent service than the mere written word. Whether you endeavour to learn by spoken or by printed instructions, you will never achieve success without constant practice on your own account; and though the fingers of an expert will in five minutes make clear what you may never have been able to understand from a book, the latter, if supplied by good diagrams, will be quite sufficiently helpful in enabling you to acquire familiarity with and ultimately proficiency in the handling of silks, furs, and feathers.

The difficulty, however, is to be able to record in writing the various manipulations in concise and unequivocal terms—a difficulty which, I must confess, has been very forcibly borne in upon me while writing these pages, and which, had I realized it in the first instance, would undoubtedly have made me think twice before undertaking to write a book on fly-dressing at all, particularly in view of other and routine work on hand which left me only a few moments at odd times to devote to what under different circumstances would have been a form of amusement.

Though I have been at considerable pains to make my meaning clear and to avoid ambiguity throughout, I am by no means happy in my mind that I have succeeded in doing so. But I venture to hope that any deficiencies

that will be found in the text will be made
good by the black and white drawings which
illustrate it, and for the excellence of which
I am indebted to the artist, Mr. St. Barbe
Goldsmith, to whom it is my agreeable duty
to take this opportunity of publicly recording my sense of obligation for the trouble he
has taken to give effect to those points
which appeared to me of particular importance.

The fly-dressing part proper of the book
begins at Chapter IV., and if the reader is
essentially of a practical turn of mind, and is
desirous of avoiding what will no doubt appear
to him unnecessary verbiage, I would recommend him to skip the first three chapters.

I may, perhaps, mention that I never had
a lesson in fly-dressing in my life. Moreover,
such books purporting to deal with the subject
as I was able to secure, were all of them either
insufficient or more or less unintelligible to
me. If he thinks this book fails to supply the
deficiency, or what I imagine to be a deficiency
(and that in fact was one of the objects with
which the book was written), the reader may,
perhaps, derive some consolation from the fact

that I succeeded in learning to dress flies under a similar disadvantage !

All the flies illustrated in this book —both coloured and uncoloured illustrations—were (with two exceptions, which I have mentioned) dressed by myself ; and though I am far from being an expert, it would be idle to imply that they would not pass muster before practical salmon fishermen of experience. I am, however, well aware that the real expert will be able to detect in the coloured plates those flies which show undoubted blemishes, and perhaps to trace therefrom, equally as well as I can, the flies which were dressed nearly two years ago and those which were dressed only a few weeks back.

I cannot conclude without emphasizing the enormous advantage derived in merely watching an expert fly-dresser at work. Some time ago I had the privilege of looking over the shoulder of Mr. William McNicol—an expert " salmon man " as well as an expert salmon fly-dresser, who includes me among a large circle of appreciators in England as well as in Scotland and elsewhere—while he dressed four of the most difficult types of fly met with—viz., a Spey Fly, a Durham Ranger, a Jock Scott, and a Silver Doctor, and I can safely say that I gleaned more " tips " in that brief space of time than I would have done in many months, perhaps years, either by reading books or by relying upon my own unaided individual activities. *Verbum sat sapienti.*

T. E. P.-T.

PART ONE

HOW TO DRESS SALMON FLIES

CHAPTER I

BY WAY OF JUSTIFICATION ON GENERAL GROUNDS

Is there any advantage in being able to dress your own salmon flies ? The answer is Yes, undoubtedly.

Do the advantages more than compensate for the time and trouble necessary to acquire proficiency ? The answer is again Yes, unless the individual is the unfortunate possessor of congenitally and impossibly clumsy fingers.

Let me endeavour to substantiate these replies.

Salmon fishing nowadays, with the demand ever in excess of the supply, is admittedly an expensive luxury.

Salmon flies are also an expensive luxury, but where hundreds of pounds are spent in rents, there is not much reason to grumble at the few score pounds expended towards as complete and representative a collection of these somewhat exotic adornments to every proper salmon fisher's kit, and therefore, at first sight, there would not, perhaps, appear to be much of a case in favour of tying your own flies on the score of economy, though it may, I think, be taken as an undoubted fact that the home-made fly does mean a saving of money.

Economy, however, is not the whole or the main consideration, for to be able to dress salmon flies, and to do it well, is much more satisfactory in many important respects than to have to depend upon the work of others.

One does not by any means wish to imply that the shop-tied fly is unsatisfactory. Far from it. Indeed, when it is realized that not one in fifty of the individuals employed in the trade are practical salmon anglers, or have the slightest interest in the future existence of the flies they turn out, it is rather wonderful that shop-tied patterns are as good as they are.

But for all that, there is an indescribable *something* about a fly dressed by an expert amateur, who is a practical salmon fisherman, which the fly dressed by a non-angling professional not infrequently lacks. I have heard this peculiar quality rather neatly referred to as " soul." A precise explanation of what is meant by " soul " is one of the impossibilities. The term is incomprehensible to the uninitiated, but is completely understood by the experienced man. Salmon fishing is full of these incommunicable significances.

Then again, it is a distinct advantage to be independent of the shop-tied fly when away on a fishing expedition. You may be many miles away from civilization—say in Norway—and discover that a certain pattern or (more important, perhaps) a certain size of a certain pattern is not to be found in your fly-book. It is unnecessary to point out how easily and quickly the gap can be filled by manufacturing the desired article oneself on the spot, or, on the other hand, how precious days may be wasted by having to wait for its delivery by your tackle maker, prompt and reliable though he may be.

Lastly, though not least, we must not forget that inasmuch as dressing salmon flies is an art, it is therefore also a hobby. It is an agreeable way of giving expression to one's sense of the artistic, and there must be few educated people who do not possess that sense to a certain degree. It gives the hands an innocent and a useful occupation during the close season, and at other periods of forced inaction, and the mind a restful change from much reading. Gaps made in the pages of the fly-book during the past season can be filled in, new patterns evolved, perhaps, and old patterns mended or varied. With it all there is a pride in achieving something tangible, commensurate, though in humbler degree, with that of the painter or sculptor. And there is added to it the pleasure of being able to give one's handiwork to a brother angler in need, who usually appreciates the gift the more by reason of its being the work of the giver. Many valuable and lasting friendships have originated thus.

For all these reasons I would most certainly advocate the practical salmon fisher to learn to tie his own flies. He may rest assured that his angling will not suffer thereby, and that the charm of his hobby will undoubtedly be enhanced.

CHAPTER II

CONSIDERABLE divergence of opinion—reasoned and otherwise—exists on the subject of salmon flies. But it is not my intention to attempt an analysis of the position—here at any rate.

I should like, however, to take the opportunity of emphasizing one or two points in connection with salmon flies, and of drawing attention to the desirability—and the possibility—of evolving some sort of order out of what is, too often, a somewhat chaotic state of affairs, my object being to help the reader to grasp the significance of salmon flies generally by ultimately presenting him with a classification of salmon flies on a practical basis.

The reader, if he be a trout fisher, must, of course, at the outset entirely dissociate from his mind any analogy of the salmon fly to the trout fly, *quâ* fly. The trout fly is

5

usually, more or less, an imitation of some natural insect upon which trout feed. Whether it achieves that object is a matter of opinion, but at any rate the intention is there. The salmon fly, however, imitates Heaven alone knows what, and if it does in certain instances bear a remote (and rather glorified) resemblance to some insect, the circumstance is the result of accident and not intention. It is true the general form of a salmon fly is that of many trout flies, but this fact merely indicates its genesis, so to speak, from the latter, and does not necessarily convey any intention that its interpretation by salmon should be similar to that which is presumably adopted by trout in regard to the trout fly proper.

It has been suggested as a convenient compromise that salmon flies should be called "lures." But an artificial minnow or a spoon are equally "lures," and the adoption of that term would lead to misunderstandings at once. On the whole, it seems best to adhere to the old-established term salmon fly, with a mental reservation that there is no analogy to the trout fly.

The trout fisher, accustomed to study the subject of flies with the spectacles of an amateur entomologist, will probably be at a loss to understand how it is possible to classify salmon flies on any reasonably practical basis.

That it is possible I will endeavour to show.

In any case, however, the fact must be borne in mind that, whatever its form, a classification of salmon flies must, from the nature of things, be a somewhat artificial affair. It can have no parallel to Nature, and is in other respects open to the objection that it is very largely dependent upon personal considerations.

Salmon flies are most conveniently grouped according to their " character," and here I should like to point out that for our purpose it is well to draw a distinction between " character " and " style."

Character in a salmon fly implies a peculiarity of shape and general construction, which is so constant and typical that it claims recognition throughout a numerous series of flies, varying, it may be considerably, from each other in size and colour, and as such divides them naturally into common groups or classes.

The essential quality which determines character is the manner in which the materials are put on.

As concrete examples of flies differing widely from each other in character we can mention—

(*a*) The Jock Scott—a built-wing with a jointed floss body. (See Plate I.)

(*b*) The Akroyd—a Dee strip-wing with a fur body. (See Plate VI.)

(*c*) The Jungle Hornet—a wingless pattern or grub with a crewel or Berlin wool body. (See Plate VII.)

Each one of these is typical of particular and distinct groups of pattern.

Style, however, is invariably referable to one particular pattern. It depends upon (i.) the relative quantity of material with which, or (ii.) the style of hook on which, a fly is dressed.

On Plate II. examples are shown which illustrate this.

The two lowest patterns are Claret Jays. Both are dressed on precisely similar hooks, and with precisely similar materials; but it will be noticed that the fly on the right has a great deal more dressing than the one on the left. The right-hand fly was tied for Lough

Melvin (by Rogan), where it is the practice to fish close to the surface. It will readily be imagined that a fly with such a quantity of dressing would tend to fish close to the surface. The other pattern, however, is dressed rather sparingly, and is applicable to fine clear waters, and where it is an advantage that the fly should fish fairly deep.

These are examples illustrating how it is possible to vary the style of a pattern by varying the quantity of material.

The two higher illustrations are Silver Greys. Here it will be observed that the *hooks* differ from each other in style, and though they are both the same length (viz., 2 inches), their dissimilarity of proportion has the effect of making the one appreciably heavier than the other, even though the amount of " dress " may be the same in each pattern. The most obvious application of this kind of style variation is when it is necessary to use a big fly, but at the same time desirable to keep it light.

So much for " style."

Now, although " character " provides a very convenient basis for classification, there are other considerations to be taken into account before it is possible to group salmon flies in such a manner as to meet with the requirements of the fly-dresser and angler alike; for I am assuming that the reader is, or desires to

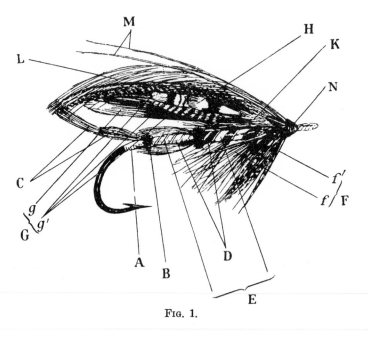

Fig. 1.

be, both. In addition, therefore, to characteristics which present marked differences from a technical point of view, and which in consequence primarily concern the fly-dresser, we must take into account certain features which, though they do affect the fly-dresser to a certain extent, have a more direct bearing upon the angler. For instance, the necessity of the grouping together under a separate heading of what are known as small summer patterns illustrates my point.

But before considering any general classification, it is, perhaps, a necessary thing to draw attention to the " anatomical parts," so to speak, of the individual fly, and for our model we will take the Jock Scott, which is one of the most elaborately constructed patterns in existence (Fig. 1).

A is the Tag.—*Tags* may be of (i.) tinsel (oval or flat), (ii.) thread, or (iii.) twist—gold or silver—(*a*) plain, or (*b*) combined with floss silk (most commonly), or wool, or fur. Floss silk is most pleasing to the eye in the dry state, but wool shows up better and keeps its colour better in water.

B is the Butt.—*Butts* may be (i.) of herl (Ostrich or Peacock, the former dyed any colour you please, if not the natural black), or (ii.) wool—of all colours.

C is the Tail.—The basis of practically all *tails* is a Golden Pheasant topping. This is by

B

reason of the fact that this particular
feather has a fine translucent brilliance,
and possesses a natural and convenient
upward curve, which gives a neat and
attractive finish.   In addition to the
topping, many tails have other feathers
combined therewith, the most commonly
employed being the orange breast feathers
of the Indian Crow, strands of Golden
Pheasant tippet and red breast feather,
Summer Duck, Teal, dyed Swan, Gallina,
Cock of the Rock, and Red Ibis feathers.
Personally I attach considerable importance to the tail, and consider that a
brilliant transparency is a most important
feature.

D is the Body.—*Bodies* admit of considerable variety, but the most prevalent
are of—

(i.) Fur (either plain, or shaded, or contrasted).

(ii.) Floss silk (either plain, or shaded,
or contrasted).

(iii.) Tinsel (either gold or silver—flat,
oval, or embossed ; and they may be
throughout of the same kind of tinsel, or

they may be divided up into two or more kinds).

Any of these may be combined one with another (*e.g.*, tinsel with fur, fur with silk, silk with tinsel), and they may have two or more joints—*i.e.*, butted with herl, and veiled with certain feathers, such as Indian Crow and Toucan breast feathers ; or the joints may be just simply separated from each other by a few turns of hackle, as in the majority of grubs.

Bodies of silk and tinsel are very commonly jointed. Less commonly bodies are made of crewel, Berlin wool, natural fur, Peacock herl, Ostrich herl, or quill.

E is the Ribbing.—The *ribbing* is practically always of tinsel in any of its varieties. In flies ribbed with flat tinsel and possessing a body hackle, twist is used as well, and is wound behind the tinsel as a protection to the hackle.

F is the Hackle—(*f* being the body or *ribbing hackle*, *f'* the *throat hackle*, or just simply the *throat*).—Some flies have only a throat hackle, others have a ribbing hackle as well, and in these the throat may be of a totally different colour to the ribbing hackle. Sometimes there are two throat hackles. Usually the hackles are domestic cock's hackles, and more often than not these are dyed. Throat hackles, however, are very commonly what are termed coarse-fibred feathers—*e.g.*, Gallina, Teal, Jay.

The Spey cock's hackle is a peculiarity which must be regarded as an exception, both in character and in the manner in which it is put on.

Heron hackles (grey and black), and feathers from the thigh of the Golden Eagle (dyed and natural), are very frequently used as ribbing hackles in the Dee strip-wing patterns.

G is the Wing—(*g* being the *under wing*, *g* the *upper* or *covering wing*).—From the fact that the wing is the most difficult part of the salmon fly to dress, and that it admits of the greatest amount of variation, both in colouring, quality, quantity, and method of putting on, it is generally regarded as the most characteristic feature in salmon flies, and through it and on it a classification of patterns can be and has largely been based. The different varieties are :

(i.) *Ordinary or Simple Strip-Wings.*— These may be set on (*a*) with an upright inclination, or (*b*) more or less on a slant. The kind of feather used as well as the manner in which it is put on will influence the set of this variety of wing. For instance, the uprightness of a wing will vary according to whether the feathers composing it are stiff fibred (*e.g.*, Turkey tail, Bustard) or soft fibred (*e.g.*, Mallard, Teal), and it will also depend upon whether "right" and "left" strips are employed for the wings of the corresponding or the opposite sides. Similarly the slanting character or droop of a wing is enhanced by using "right" and "left" strips of a soft-fibred feather, such as Mallard, to form the right and left wings respectively, as, for example, in the Spey flies, in which drooping wings are to be seen in their most pronounced form.*

* Throughout this book the terms "right" and "left," as applied to strips and fibres, will frequently recur, and

As regards the manner in which the wings are put on and the influence this has upon the general effect, the accompanying diagram (Fig. 2) may perhaps help to make things clear. Imagine that a transverse section of the hook-shank has been made at the point where the wings are to be tied in, and that this section, being roughly a circle, is divided by vertical and transverse diameters, AB and CD respectively, into quadrants. The vertical diameter AB represents the "middle line" of the hook, and will be referred to again on several occasions

it will be as well to explain here what is precisely implied thereby.

If you take the centre tail feather of any bird (say a common Pheasant) and hold it in front of you for examination by the stem with the tip pointing upwards and the "best" side towards you—as you naturally would do—you would regard the fibres to the right of you as being "right side" fibres, and those to the left as "left side" fibres. Although, zoologically speaking, I believe this is incorrect, nevertheless for fly-dressing purposes it is most convenient, and I will therefore assume that every mention of the terms "right" and "left" in speaking of fibres for winging will have reference to this incorrect but convenient interpretation in respect of all feathers, whether tail (centre or otherwise), or wing, or body feathers.

later on. It bisects the hook longitudinally into equal and similar halves. The
transverse diameter *CD* also bisects the
hook, but not into equal and similar
halves. It represents the "lateral line."

Now, speaking generally and ignoring
for the moment the importance of the

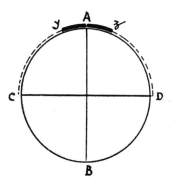

FIG. 2.

kind of feather used, uprightness in wings
is secured by tying in both wings at the
same time on the top of the hook-shank,
and in such a way that each wing rests on
its corresponding side of the middle line,
and only occupies at the point where
it is tied in a very small portion of the
arc *AC* or *AD*, as the case may be

(viz., the arcs Ay and Az). The fibres
of the strips are pressed together by the
dressing silk in much the same way as
the folds of an accordion-pleated material
can be pressed together, and the strips
themselves lie in the same plane to the
hook as a whole.

Slanting wings, however, are tied in
each separately, and in such a way that
they occupy the entire arcs AC and AD
respectively. The fibres in this case are
not pressed *together* by the dressing silk,
but each individual one is pressed on to
the hook-shank. This explains why in
this style of winging it is not always
easy to maintain the coherence of the
strip as a whole, as the natural relation-
ship of the fibres to each other is apt
to be disturbed, and the strip accordingly
splits. Some feathers (*e.g.*, Turkey tails)
will not submit to this method of tying
in without splitting, and they therefore
require a special treatment, which is set
forth in Chapter **XIV**.

In every case and in all styles of
winging it is most important that each

wing should keep to its corresponding side of the middle line.

(ii.) *Whole-Feather Wings.*—These are composed of entire feathers (*e.g.*, Golden Pheasant tippet and sword feather, Jungle Cock neck) set on upright in pairs, back to back.*

(iii.) *Mixed-Wings*, which are made up of a number of single strands of various feathers "married" to each other in one continuous "sheath."

(iv.) *Built-Wings.*†—These have as a

* By "back to back" is meant the direct apposition of the under or inner surfaces—*i.e.*, the outer or "best" surfaces showing on each side.

† The distinction between "mixed" and "built" wings is in practice rather a fine one. Strictly speaking, a mixed-wing is composed of a number of single strips of several different kinds of feather. Not uncommonly these are tied on in a bunch anyhow, but usually all the fibres are carefully "married" one to another in a certain definite order. The appearance of a carefully mixed wing gives one the impression of a Persian carpet—a conglomeration of a multitude of colours.

A built-wing, on the other hand, is constructed on bolder lines, and the essential thing about it is, that instead of being tied on all at once, it is *built* in stages, one portion above another, but in such a manner that, like the tiles of a roof, the portions underneath are left exposed by those immediately above them. Very often foundation either a plain wing of paired upright strips or a whole-feather wing. Over this " married " fibres of several sorts of feathers are superimposed in batches of two or more.

(v.) *Topping-Wings*, in which Golden Pheasant crest feathers entirely form the wing.

(vi.) *Herl-Wings*, which are composed of strands or strips from either the tail or the sword feathers of the Peacock.

H is the Side.—*Sides* may be of Jungle Cock, Indian Crow, Summer Duck, or any other richly coloured or strongly marked feather. They occupy the central portions of the wings, leaving a strip showing both above and below, and sometimes they extend backwards as far as the butt, or where the butt ought to be.

---

the first portion is made up of broad paired strips of some plain feather (*e.g.*, white-tipped Turkey tail in Jock Scott, which is the type of a built-wing pattern), over which " married " strips of different feathers are built, but always in such a way as to leave a portion of the first pair visible. An artistically constructed built-wing gives a very pleasing effect, but it tends to bulk, and is therefore not as a rule suitable for small flies.

K is the Cheek.—*Cheeks* are commonly of Jungle Cock, Blue Chatterer, or Indian Crow. They are superimposed upon the sides (where these occur), and are quite short. In some flies (*e.g.*, the Akroyd) they are tied on so as to droop.

L is the Topping.—The *topping* is invariably from the Golden Pheasant's crest. The effect of a properly shaped and properly adjusted topping is to keep the wings together, and also to produce a glistening transparency to the upper edge of the wing, which is most effective in bright weather.

M represents the Horns.—*Horns* are usually obtained from the tail feather of the Macaw, and may be blue and yellow, blue and red, or scarlet—single strands of the feather being used as a rule. They constitute an element of mobility in a fly, and mechanically are useful in protecting brittle, delicate feathers, such as Jungle Cock, when these latter are used as cheeks or sides. They are usually put on last of all and over the topping.*

* With the foregoing as a guide the reader will perhaps be in a position to understand the description of a pattern

Having thus considered the anatomical parts of salmon flies generally, the reader will now perhaps be in a position to grasp the main points in the following classification, which has been drawn up after due consideration of the fly-dresser and angler alike.

Salmon flies seem to fall naturally into six great groups—viz., (I.) General flies, (II.) Dee

---

from written directions. For the Jock Scott—our model— the dressing may be given thus:

Tag.—Silver tinsel (oval).

Butt.—Ostrich herl (black).

Tail.—A topping and Indian Crow (laid on flat, best surface uppermost).

Body.—Jointed in two equal halves. Posterior joint of lemon floss ribbed with fine silver tinsel (oval), butted with (black) Ostrich herl, and veiled above and below with Toucan Anterior joint of black floss ribbed with broader oval or flat tinsel (in the latter case reinforced with twist), and a natural black domestic cock's hackle.

Throat.—Gallina.

Wings.—Two strips of black white-tipped Turkey tail set on back to back; over these married fibres of yellow Swan, Florican, scarlet Swan, Bustard, grey Turkey tail, and Golden Pheasant tail; over these a strand of Peacock sword feather and married strips of Teal and Summer Duck; and over all a strip of brown Mallard.

Sides.—Jungle Cock.

Cheeks.—Blue Chatterer.

Topping.—Golden Pheasant crest.

Horns.—Blue and yellow Macaw over all.

strip-wing flies, (III.) Spey flies, (IV.) Grubs, (V.) Irish patterns, (VI.) Small summer patterns.

I. *General Flies* (see Plates I., III., IV., and V.) may themselves be subdivided into six classes—viz. :

(i.) Simple strip-wings — *e.g.*, Dreadnought, March Brown, Thunder and Lightning, and all patterns approximating to the sea trout or loch type in which the features are those of ordinary winged brown trout flies.

(ii.) Whole-feather wings—*e.g.*, Orange Parson, Durham Ranger, Candlestick Maker.

(iii.) Mixed-wings—*e.g.*, Popham, Silver Doctor, Silver Grey.

(iv.) Built - wings — *e.g.*, Jock Scott, Butcher, Dusty Miller.

(v.) Topping-wings—*e.g.*, Canary, Black Prince.

(vi.) Herl-wings—*e.g.*, Green Peacock, Beauly Snowfly.

And the bodies of these may be of any of the varieties already discussed.

This comprises the biggest group, and from every point of view is the most important. Besides the most popular and most costly patterns, it includes some of the most difficult to dress—*e.g.*, Durham Ranger, Silver Grey, Popham, Jock Scott. Incidentally, it is as a group the most gaudy. It may, in fact, be regarded as the salmon fisherman's " show ' regiment, and when exhibited to fair feminine eyes will invariably elicit the gratifying exclamation, " Oh, how lovely !" Some of the more brilliant are much affected by beginners, both on their casts and in their head gear (the latter situation being perhaps the more important of the two from the point of view of effect).

By reason of their general applicability the flies coming under this group are very commonly referred to as " standard " patterns, meaning thereby that no matter what the local conditions may be, one or other of these general flies will give a good account of itself in use when tested side by side with the special or particular patterns fashionable locally.

II. *Dee Strip-Winged Flies* (see Plate VI.).—These are a very distinct group, being peculiar in their appearance, and somewhat limited in their seasonal and geographical application. They originate from that queen of salmon rivers, the Aberdeenshire Dee, and are one of the oldest types of patterns still surviving.

They are extensively used for the early spring or late winter fishing in those clear, cold rivers of the north - eastern portion of Scotland, where they are very popular for many reasons, not the least important of which being their cheapness. (This is a by no means subordinate consideration, as anyone who has fished in a blustering spring gale can fully testify.)

In the early part of the season, when the temperature of the water is not far removed from freezing-point, " Dee strip-wings " are used dressed on very large irons, 3 inches being a not uncommon length.* These unusually large sizes are found expedient for the reason that, owing to the lightness of their dressing, the flies sink deeper, and are therefore more likely to come within the range of vision of fish

* Mr. Kelson, in " Tips," speaks of having dressed them on 6-inch irons, and killing fish therewith.

which, when the temperature of the water is low, will be lying close to the bottom.

As a matter of fact, these exceptionally large patterns do not appear outrageously big, because, in addition to the lightness of their dressing, they are, as a general rule, sombre in colouring. Their appearance does not scandalize our sense of propriety, and, more important, they do not tend to scare the fish for which they are intended.

In addition to their suitability for the particular circumstances in view, they possess an attractive feature in the extreme mobility of their hackles and wings, which imparts a very life-like appearance to the fly as it works in the water.

Altogether, it will be seen that this is essentially a practical type of pattern, exemplifying the importance of use over ornament, and as such somewhat in contrast to the preceding group.

III. *Spey Flies* (see Plate VII.).—These are even more peculiar-looking than the preceding. The shortness of the wings, and the unusual manner in which these are put on, produce a sort of hump-backed effect, which looks rather wicked. They are out of the ordinary in every respect. The bodies are short, and have no adornments in the shape of tag, tail, or butt; and are usually composed of crewels or Berlin wools of various and varying colours, put on as sparingly as possible. The ribbing tinsel is individually broad and collectively plentiful, and, as often as not, besides thread and twist, gold and silver tinsel are used on one and the same body. The hackles are long and very mobile. Both grey and black Heron hackles are used, but the hackle of a typical Spey fly is obtained from the lateral tail feathers of a certain breed of domestic fowl, known as the " Spey-cock." These are not easy to procure. The method of putting them on is contrary to the general rule, as they are tied in base first instead of tip first—*i.e.*, the longest fibres are at the tail end of the fly— and they are sometimes wound round the body in the reverse way to the tinsel, a piece of twist or fine oval tinsel being wound on last over the hackle, to prevent it from getting torn by the fishes' teeth. As a matter of fact, the direction in which the hackle is wound will depend upon which side of it is stripped, for only one side is used, and accordingly it may go with or against the body tinsel; but the retaining twist or tinsel will, of course, always go in a direction opposite to that of the hackle, and therefore it may go, according to circumstances, with or against the body tinsel, in which latter event a further unusual effect is produced.   The wings are almost invariably plain brown Mallard strips, " right " sides being used for right wings, and *vice versa.* The natural curve of the fibres of this feather enhances the drooping character of the wings.

The Spey fly is a somewhat unique production.   It is not every salmon fisherman who has used a Spey fly, or who even knows what it looks like; I have therefore thought it worth while to include the foregoing remarks, as being possibly of some use.*

* I am indebted to Messrs. William Brown, of Aberdeen (of Browns' Phantom fame), for their kindness in sending me patterns actually tied by Spey-side gillies to copy from.   From them I elicited the information that there was no such thing as a constant dressing of any Spey fly, for the reason that every dresser had a different rendering for each pattern, and, moreover, subjected his own rendering to considerable variation. I might mention that none of the patterns depicted on Plate VII. are precisely the same in detail as the similarly

Although, beyond the limits of Spey-side, one never hears much mention of Spey flies, nevertheless, Messrs. Farlow tell me that they sell a great number every season for use elsewhere than on the Spey, so it would seem that they enjoy a certain measure of general popularity ; and, indeed, there is no reason why they should not kill elsewhere than on the Spey, on waters having a similar character to that river.

IV. *Grubs* (see Plate VII.).—These are merely glorified palmers—glorified in the sense that they are as a rule much larger and almost invariably more ornamented than the trouting editions. They form a comparatively small group, and come into action more especially in warm weather, the inference being that as they resemble to a certain—and one must confess somewhat remote—degree caterpillars prevalent in summer and early autumn, they should be used under those conditions when it might be expected that the living counterpart comes before the notice of salmon !

---

named patterns sent to me by Messrs. Brown, thus adding point to the statement that there does not exist such a thing as a constant dressing of any Spey fly !

Grubs are the easiest patterns to tie, not being possessed of those troublesome adjuncts, the wings. The beginner would be well advised to make his first attempts on this class of fly, as the results will be more encouraging to him, and at the same time nothing will be lost from the point of view of educating the fingers in the proper manipulation of silk, fur, tinsel, and feather.

V. *Irish Patterns** (see Plate VIII.) are merely general patterns, possessing as a rule rather more wing and more variety of colour in the wing than those coming under the first group of this classification. They have a very common feature in the shape of Mallard strips partly veiling the mixed-wing underneath, and very few of them have the adornment of a topping over the wing.† Though they are not as brilliant as the usual Scotch type of fly,

* This, together with the following class, is somewhat supplementary to the four preceding ones—which may be regarded as the four natural groups into which it is possible to divide salmon flies—and are added more for the benefit of the angler, as they have a very definite sphere of influence in practice.

† Where toppings do occur, however, there is no stint of them—*e.g.*, Orange Parson, a type of pattern which claims origin from the north-west of Ireland.

they give an impression of greater warmth of colouring, a richer general effect, the bodies being very often varied and shaded in pleasing and harmonious schemes of colour.   They seem to be peculiarly well suited to peaty waters, and, from the quantity of wing they possess — relatively speaking — it is safe to assume that they do not fish as deep as some other types of fly.

VI. *Small Summer Patterns* (see Plate IX.). —These can be of any, or all, of the types recognized, and are in the main small editions of the regular salmon flies.   They are very often dressed on small double hooks, and the materials are sparingly used.   Late spring. summer, and early autumn is their seasonal range, and low clear waters and fine settled weather the conditions of their use.

They form a fascinating group, as they require considerable artistic skill and manipulative dexterity to turn out satisfactorily.

So much for the salmon fly, as such, and its classification.

The reader may be inclined to grumble, perhaps not without justification, at this long preamble, but I am assuming that he does not know " all about it " ; and I am hoping that it may serve the purpose of encouraging the formation of an orderly mind, which is such a necessary adjunct to an orderly method, and which in its turn is so essential for approaching the subject of fly-dressing in a methodical manner.

At all events, the foregoing may be skipped by those who do know " all about it," as I have been careful to intimate in the preface.

CHAPTER III

HOOKS

THE purpose of the hook is primarily, of course, to connect the salmon firmly and securely to the angler.

It, however, performs another function, for, by varying its relative proportions and the thickness of its iron, it has considerable influence upon the practical effect of the pattern dressed on it. This point has already been touched upon in the preceding chapter when discussing " style."

It is not my intention—nor should I be able—to give a lengthy dissertation on the mechanical principles underlying the act of hooking. That has already been done by other and more capable writers. But it may not, perhaps, be out of place to mention a few points which occur to me as being of practical importance. They need not detain us long.

If the point of a hook which has been attached to a piece of gut is lightly fixed into the edge of a cork or soft deal board, with the shank of the hook parallel to the surface of the board, and a pull is given to the gut (which, for the purpose in view, must also be kept parallel to the surface of the board), the tip of the shank will at once dip down and touch the board. This position is regarded as the one invariably assumed by a hook at the moment of " engagement "—*i.e.*, the moment when the hook grasped in the salmon's mouth is subjected to the opposing forces represented respectively by the uplifting of the rod-point on the part of the angler and the downward-moving bulk of the salmon, aided by the volume and momentum of the water pressing against it. Accordingly, the correctness of the mechanical construction of a hook is generally criticized by reference to this position, which is represented diagrammatically by joining the tips of shank and point together by a straight line, which is subsequently produced at each extremity (see the line *AB* in Figs. 3, 4, 5, and 6).

It appears to be generally admitted that the

FIG. 3.

FIG. 4.

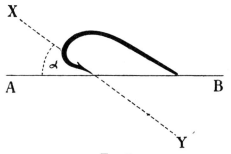

FIG. 5.

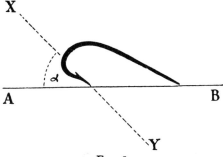

FIG. 6.

assumption on which this method of estimating
the mechanical correctness of a hook is based
is a reasonable one.

Now, it seems to me that the mechanics
of hooking resolves itself into questions of
(1) *promptness of engagement*, and (2) *depth
of penetration*, involved with both of which,
but subordinate to each, being (3) *ease of
penetration*.

The late H. P. Wells, in his admirable book
' Fly Rods and Fly Tackle," by an ingenious
illustration, suggested how the significance of
these principles could most readily be appreciated.   He asked you to compare the different
results achieved in working an ordinary car-
penter's chisel upon a block of wood, first
with the straight surface of the chisel uppermost, and secondly with the bevelled surface
uppermost.   The results are worth considering in some detail, for there is a rather close
analogy between the blade of the chisel and
the point of a hook.

The chisel with the straight surface of the
blade placed uppermost, and with the bevel
laid parallel with the surface of the board, will
not bite.   It represents the point of a hook,

the direction of which exactly coincides with the line *AB* (see Fig. 3). Such a hook will never engage properly.

The chisel with the bevelled surface of the blade placed uppermost will bite, but the extent to which it will bite depends upon the angle at which the blade is inclined. The more steeply the blade is inclined the deeper will it bite ; but a stage is reached at which the edge, instead of biting, merely scrapes along the surface of the wood. This represents the point of a hook the direction of which is outside the line *AB* (Figs. 4, 5, and 6). The depth of engagement will depend upon the size of the angle formed by the line *AB* and the line representing the direction of the point. This angle is sometimes referred to as the *angle of impact* (*a* in Figs. 4, 5, and 6). Within certain limits, the larger this angle is the deeper will be the penetration.

The blade of the chisel may be inclined so as to shave off either fine or coarse parings. So long as it continues to shave off parings, it represents the point of a hook with a very small angle of impact. Such a point engages, but does not penetrate deeply, though it penetrates *easily* (see Fig. 4).

As soon, however, as the blade of the chisel is inclined so that it ceases to shave off parings, but bites deeper and deeper into the wood and jambs, then we have a representation of a hook point with a large angle of impact. Such a point not only engages at once, but penetrates deeply, and the larger the angle of impact the deeper (within certain limits) will be the penetration, *but the less easy* the penetration (see Fig. 5).

Finally, the blade may be so inclined that, though the bevelled surface is still uppermost, it does not bite at all, but merely scrapes along the surface of the wood. In this case it represents the point of a hook which has a very large angle of impact—in fact, almost a right angle. It will neither engage nor penetrate, and we have the same result observed in our first illustration, though produced by totally different causes (see Fig. 6).

Though it by no means disposes of the question, I think that the above homely illustration will serve to indicate the principles to observe and the features to avoid in a hook.

Ease of penetration, as I have already suggested, is a subordinate consideration, being very largely dependent on the sharpness of the point (which should always emulate the needle) and the gradient of the barb (which should always be an easy one). But promptness of engagement and deep penetration are of primary importance, and I am inclined to think that these two essential qualities in a hook are almost entirely governed by the direction of the point, and therefore by the size of the angle of impact, which, in my own opinion, should not be less than 20 degrees, or exceed 45 degrees.

Whatever the general shape of the hook may be, I think that a point turned slightly out—*i.e.*, away from the shank—is a distinct advantage. This must not, of course, be overdone, and it should always be checked by reference to the angle of impact, which, by the way, is very directly influenced by the length of the shank, as well as by the direction of the point—a fact which is demonstrable on any hook.*

* *Ceteris paribus*, the angle of impact increases in size as the shank decreases in length.

In addition to the foregoing considerations, common sense will point to the desirability of the existence of a reasonably large interval between barb and bend, so as to insure a good hold after the point has penetrated.

As to shape, I do not think that there is much to choose between the old round bend and the Limerick. The latter is usually regarded as being somewhat stronger, though I am unable to see on what grounds. Personally, I use Limericks, because they are more suited to the shape of the conventional salmon fly than is the round bend.

The Sproat is by some still regarded as the best form of hook in existence, but it seems to me that the advantage claimed for it is based on a totally erroneous premise—viz., that ease of penetration is the most important feature in a hook. It is not an elegant shape.

As for snecked hooks, you would be well advised in giving them a wide berth.

A word now as to thickness of iron and general proportion.

It may be said, as a general rule, that the heavier the iron, within reason, the better, because, in the first place, it implies strength ;

and in the second, it means that the fly dressed on it will fish deep.

But though the principle of a heavy iron is a sound one, it must not be carried to extremes. Its expediency in the larger size of hooks, for instance, will be called into question.   Except on rivers like the Tay, where most of the fishing with large flies is by harling, big, heavy irons are not only inexpedient, but impracticable.   Accordingly, for casting, when the necessity for a big fly arises, it is almost invariably the rule to use hooks which, while producing a large size of fly, at the same time reduce weight and bulk to the minimum by increasing the length of the shank out of the usual proportion to the bend.   These are known as " long Dees," so called, presumably, because they are regarded as originating from the Aberdeenshire Dee, where it is rather uncommon to see any other kind of hook used ; but it is probable that the Spey is equally responsible for their genesis.

The use of the " long Dee " is not necessarily confined to the large sizes.   Wherever a light, flimsy type of pattern is required, or whenever a fly comparatively large as to length of

" dress " must be used on fairly light gut and a grilse rod, the principle of the " long Dee " applies.

Now, as to a range of sizes—*i.e.*, a practical range that will meet with every requirement likely to arise—and in this connection I cannot refrain from indulging in a growl. It is impossible to be a salmon fisherman or a flydresser for any length of time without having it very forcibly borne in upon one that there is very urgent need for some rational, uniform, and universal system of grading hooks. The perfectly illogical and erratic manner in which every different hook maker seeks to establish his own scale, without a thought for the practical requirements of his ultimate customers, would be laughable if it were not so exceedingly irritating.

Every-day instances of the inconvenience and misunderstandings that arise out of the present unsatisfactory state of affairs are within the experience of most people who have anything to do with either the sale or purchase of tackle.

It is rather curious that the retail trade has not made a serious attempt to insist upon the adoption by hook manufacturers of a universally applicable standardization of hooks. It would seem to be so particularly to be desired from their point of view.

Hook manufacturers, it appears, are a peculiar and very independent class of people, and I have been told in several quarters that attempts to standardize hooks on a common-sense basis would not meet with encouragement from the people who are responsible for their manufacture. The reason for this is wrapped in the profoundest obscurity.

Nevertheless, I have been able—after no little trouble, it is true—through the good offices of Mr. John Forrest, of 24, Thomas Street, London, W., to get hooks made which are not only of unimpeachable shape and general quality, but are graded in a uniform, logical, and intelligible series.

The idea was to replace the whole confused and confusing system of notation by one which would have no reference whatever to numbers or letters, but only to definite measurements in terms of inches. There may be—and under the circumstances it is quite natural that there should be—different conceptions of the size of a hook when referred to by a certain number or symbol, but there should be no misunderstanding as to the size of a hook referred to in terms of some definite linear measurement. Whatever its demerits may be, it can at least be said that a series based on a principle such as this possesses the spirit of rationality in the sense that it does not depend upon the wholly arbitrary and inconsistent gradation of size—arranged haphazard, without any consideration for convenience or practical needs—with which the long-suffering angling public has usually to be satisfied.

At all events, I am satisfied that a standardization of salmon hooks by uniform increments in terms of inches is infinitely simpler, more intelligible, more universally applicable, and therefore more satisfactory generally, than one which depends upon a confusing and often contradictory reference to numbers or letters having no relation whatever to any measurement.

If the reader is of the same way of thinking, I invite him to look at Plates X. and XI., where these " rational " hooks—as I am pleased to call them—are to be seen. Should he desire to extend his "approval in principle" to "confirmation by use," he can procure them in any of the sizes figured at the establishment in Thomas Street already mentioned, to whose principal—viz., Mr. John Forrest, a member, it is perhaps needless to add, of the well-known Kelso firm of rod makers and tackle dealers—I am personally indebted for the very painstaking care and valuable co-operation, without which it would have been impossible to get these hooks satisfactorily made.

I must hasten to add that in drawing attention to these hooks I have no ulterior personal motives to serve, no axe to grind in the shape of concessions or royalties in the sale of the hooks, my only desire being to put the reader in the way of testing a practical series of well-made hooks, arranged on a simple and rational basis, on the assumption that he, like myself and many others, has felt the urgent need of some such series, and will not be entirely ungrateful for the information.

It will be observed that, with the exception of series D (on Plate XI.), which includes hooks for small patterns, the increment of variation is $\frac{1}{4}$ inch (which is quite small enough for all practical purposes in general salmon fishing), and that within a certain range of sizes the two styles of iron are included.

The lengths refer, of course, to the "over-all" measurements—*i.e.*, they include the bend.

The series is subdivided into four sub-groups.

Groups B and C correspond to each other in length, but differ very widely from each other in general character, group B being the long-shanked, light-ironed type, group C being the short-shanked, heavy-ironed type.

Personally, I do not admit the practicability of the heavy-ironed hook for salmon flies in sizes larger than 2 inches, except for harling, which is so far removed from fly fishing proper that it may quite justifiably be classed with trolling. Beyond 2 inches I think the type of hook should revert exclusively to the long-shanked "Dee" style, where increase of size is effected by increasing the length of the shank out of the ordinary proportion to the gape of the bend. This is the case in group A, which includes all hooks, within a practical range of sizes, which are used for early spring or late winter fishing. It is true one hears of hooks larger than 3 inches, but one very seldom

sees them, and even more seldom uses them.
On the whole, I am inclined to think that
3 inches will about meet the limit of size
required by 99 per cent. of salmon fishermen.
In group D the increment of variation is
$\frac{1}{8}$ inch. These hooks will come into use for
low summer waters.

Groups A and B are hammer hardened—*i.e.*,
the bends are flattened from side to side.
Groups C and D comprise the ordinary round-
sectioned hooks. All these hooks are, of
course, made of the very best tempered steel,
and the points are all as sharp as can be.

Eyed hooks I do not like. To be perfectly
frank, I believe this is rather unjustifiable
prejudice, because there are advantages about
them undoubtedly. Flies dressed on them
last longer, for one thing. Then they require
no gut loop, and are therefore quicker to
dress. Moreover, it is possible to dress very
thin bodies on them, an undoubted advantage
in certain cases. But they are not satisfactory
in practice, especially in the larger sizes, though,
apart from the fact that they crack off very
readily in windy weather, it is not easy to
specify their disadvantages in so many words.

I believe, however, that there is much to be said in favour of the gradual transition from a soft pliable substance like gut to a hard, comparatively unyielding material, such as the steel of a hook—a condition which is secured by the intervention of a gut loop, and which is not secured by the direct attachment of the gut casting line to a metal eye. The importance of such gradual transition becomes more marked the larger the size of hook employed.

Perhaps the greatest enemy to the eyed hook is the badly designed and badly made eye which figures on quite 99 per cent. of all eyed salmon hooks.

In the smaller sizes one must admit the convenience of eyed hooks, but the soundness of the principle of a metal eye still remains a questionable proposition—at least, I am of that opinion, though it is probably purely prejudice.

A similar prejudice exists in my mind against double hooks. In the larger sizes I cannot help thinking that it is not altogether unreasonable. There *must* be a mutually antagonistic lever-like action between the two rigidly connected hooks when fixed in a fish's mouth, with a consequent tendency to tear out, and the extra force required to drive them in at the strike is undoubtedly an objectionable feature. Small doubles — *i.e.*, less than $1\frac{1}{4}$ inches—maybe, and I am prepared to believe are, on the whole, an advantage for summer fishing, especially in naturally swift waters. Not the least advantageous points about these are that they swim well and fish deep. But I am by no means satisfied with the correctness of the principle of two hooks brazed together even in small sizes.

Admitting the convenience of eyed hooks in the smaller sizes, both single and double, for the lightly-dressed flies that are used in the fine, clear waters of the summer months, and recognizing the favours with which small double hooks are regarded by some, I had group D subdivided into four sets of hooks, each set to run concurrently one with another, and consisting of four different sizes of single and double irons respectively (see Plate XI.). The sizes run from $1\frac{1}{8}$ inches down to $\frac{6}{8}$ inch or $\frac{3}{4}$ inch (not including the eye itself), the increment of variation being $\frac{1}{8}$ inch.

The eyes are made as small as is reasonably

and safely possible, and they are inclined at an
acute angle, so that neatness of effect is produced, and the tendency to skirt and wobble
in use is to a large extent obviated.

In the double irons the eyes are brazed ; in
the single they are " re-turned " (*never* use,
either for large sea trout or for salmon, hooks
in which the eye is formed by an abruptly
finished loop).

CHAPTER IV

MATERIALS

Not the least attractive part of dressing your own flies is the collection of the materials. Indeed, it is almost a pursuit in itself—a sort of hobby within a hobby—and there are men whose chief pleasure and satisfaction seem to lie in the picking up of some particularly choice feather or skin, and who are positively loth to employ them, and so break their entirety in the actual dressing of a fly!

Now, of course, the collection of materials, especially feathers, is an endless occupation, but the practical man will draw a sharp distinction between what *should* be and what *can* be collected—in short, between what is really essential, and what is more or less superfluous. I should advise the beginner to be strictly moderate in the quantity of his collection, and he need not at first be over-particular as to

the quality, for he is bound to waste a good
deal of material; and it is better to spoil stuff
for which a great price has not been paid than
that which has cost a considerable sum of
money. Afterwards, of course, he cannot be
too particular as to the quality of his materials,
feathers especially; but for a start almost anything will do, for, after all, first attempts are
merely by the way of educating the fingers
into fine and unfamiliar movements.

Materials for salmon flies are perhaps not
so difficult to procure good as are those for
trout flies, but they are, of course, a good deal
more expensive.

A few friendly words with a poultry dealer
will as a rule result in the acquisition of a
stock of hackles, though, of course, not very
many of these will be of first-class quality,
and there will be the additional trouble and
difficulty of getting them dyed. Again, a
sporting friend is invaluable for supplying you
with desirable birds which are the victims of
his fowling-piece — viz., Woodcock, Grouse,
Partridge, Landrail, Teal, Mallard, Widgeon,
and so forth; but these come more into the
province of the trout fly-tyer, and there are

not many who can boast of a sporting friend who can furnish them with Bustard, Jungle Cock, Summer Duck, or Blue Chatterer. I only wish I possessed such a friend! Under the circumstances, one has generally to look for that particular kind of friend in a tackle shop, and he, of course, only parts with his treasures for a consideration.

The initial cost of even a modest collection of salmon-fly materials appears to many a prohibitive proposition to contemplate, and would seem to be largely responsible for the very incorrect statement that it is cheaper to buy your salmon flies ready made.

Of course, if you have the means and a bent that way, you can spend £20 over fly materials as easily as you can over equally unimportant and perhaps less harmless objects; but there is no reason why a £5 note judiciously laid out should not furnish a very workman-like outfit, both in implements and materials—as a basis, at any rate, for further developments.

There is, however, no absolute guide as to the probable cost of materials either as an initial outlay or an annual liability, and there is certainly none as to the *possible* cost. Windfalls in this, as in other matters, sometimes occur. For instance, quite recently I acquired, among other by no means negligible odds and ends in the shape of feathers and furs, forty dozen barred Summer Duck feathers for the sum of one guinea. Barred Summer Duck feathers, I should mention, for the benefit of the uninitiated, are listed at 4s. 6d. to 5s. per dozen. Even more recently I became the possessor of two of the most perfect heads and necks of Golden Pheasant I ever saw for the paltry sum of 7s. 6d. This, however, was through the influence of a "friend at court." A very useful individual is the "friend at court."

I now propose to deal briefly with the materials which the amateur can justifiably regard as meeting all reasonably practical requirements, and I will begin the list with—

HACKLES.—Hackles, from the fly-dresser's point of view, may be classed as (1) translucent, or fine-fibred—viz., cock's hackles ; (2) opaque, or coarse-fibred—*e.g.*, Teal, Gallina, and Jay ; and (3) those that do not come under either category, and are best regarded as of a special and rather exceptional nature—viz., Heron, Golden Eagle, Spey-cock.

1. *Cock's hackles* are used in their natural colours or dyed. For salmon flies the latter are more commonly employed than the former.

Natural cock's hackles in salmon flies are not used in anything like the same variety as in trout flies, and the following kinds are practically all that are really necessary — viz., furnace and cochybondhu, badger, grizzled, blue dun, rusty dun, and honey dun, red game and black. Except the duns, these are easy enough to procure, but not always easy to procure really good.

It is important to know the points of a good cock's hackle. In the first place, of course, it should be strongly marked and in the finest condition. (Three-year old birds in their mid-winter plumage furnish the best hackles.) It should be of a transparent brilliance when held up to the light, and both sides of the feather should be equally richly coloured (this is by no means common, especially in the furnace and cochybondhu varieties, which, on the under or inner surfaces, often show a dull whitish quality, which is not pleasing). Further, it should be of the proper shape—*i.e.*, the fibres at the base of the central quill should be longer than those at the tip, and there should be a gradual and uniform shortening of the fibres from base to tip, so that when they have been stroked backwards, the whole feather looks like a broad spear-head. To add that the hackle should be supple is needless, and would merely be repeating the necessity of choosing feathers from birds in good condition, those from moulting or debilitated birds being dull to look at and brittle to handle.

Furnace and *Cochybondhu* hackles are obtained from cross-bred Dorking and Red Game cocks. The furnace hackle at its best is a deep reddish-brown with a very dark brown, almost black, centre or " list." The cochybondhu is similar, with the addition of dark brown or black tips to the fibres. They are difficult to procure good in the large and small sizes, though the intermediate sizes are not so very difficult to obtain. They are chiefly used in sombre-coloured patterns, such as are used in Wales and the West Highlands of Scotland.

Badger hackles come from cross-bred Dorking cocks, and are white or creamy, with black "lists." Some have the fibres tipped with black, and are then sometimes paradoxically enough known as "white cochy-bondhu." They are very effective on bodies of black floss or silver tinsel.

Grizzled or *cuckoo* hackles are supplied by pure-bred Plymouth Rocks, and are easy enough to obtain good. They are grey, with darker grey mottlings. Some have a yellowish or brownish tinge. These are not the best.

Dun hackles—blue, rusty, and honey duns —are only found on Blue Andalusians or Blue Game cocks, and very often the same bird will have all varieties of duns. These are rather dull feathers for salmon-fly work, and are chiefly used for grubs, especially the honey-dun.

Red game are most difficult to get, of the proper rich mahogany or reddish-brown tint. A three-year-old Indian Game cock produces the richest hackles, though sometimes a red Bantam cock has some very fine ones of a smaller size. Under the generic name of "red game," all shades of cinnamon and brown are grouped, and various breeds of fowl produce them in varying shades and qualities (*e.g.*, Cochin China, Buff Orpington, and many cross-breeds), but the Indian Game is *facile princeps.*

Black (natural) cock's hackles are, perhaps, the most difficult of any to obtain good. Indeed, they are in the main so unsatisfactory that I nearly always use dyed ones, which are much deeper, and more uniform in tone. The trouble about these, however, is that the dye very often makes them brittle. *Sometimes* a Black Minorca cock will give good black hackles.

Dyed cock's hackles for salmon flies may be of every conceivable shade, but the practical dresser for his own use need not burden himself with a very large selection of colours, and he will find that the following will meet with most of his requirements : pale sky blue, turquoise blue, claret (a full rich Burgundy), magenta, scarlet (cardinal), orange (a deep boiled-prawn shade), lemon (really a sulphur yellow), green (grass green, *not* olive green), fiery brown, golden olive, purple (dark violet), and black. In addition, badger hackles, dyed lemon, orange, red, and fiery brown, come in useful at times.

I do not propose to deal with the subject of dyeing hackles or feathers of any kind. Dyeing is an art in itself, requiring a great deal of care, time, and patience to do properly. I should not advise the amateur to attempt to dye his own feathers, unless he has plenty of time and a suitable "messing" room at his disposal. It is certainly not an occupation for a civilized dwelling-house, as it produces a great deal of mess, and it will be a long time before the amateur obtains satisfactory results. In short, "the game is hardly worth the candle," and I for one prefer to get my feathers and fur already dyed from the establishments which provide them. The cost of feathers and fur dyed in the manner and in the quantity in which they are dyed at home does not work out very much cheaper than that of the purchase of those professionally dyed in bulk, and in any case the slight extra expense involved in buying the stuff ready dyed more than compensates for the time and trouble saved.

The dyeing of feathers for trout flies (dry flies especially) comes in a rather different category. Here it is a necessity, for dyed trout hackles are, comparatively speaking, costly, and not easy to obtain in the proper shades.

Cock's hackles, both natural and dyed, are commonly sold in bundles of a dozen, the usual price being 4d. per bundle. As these are picked feathers, the cost is not outrageous, and one is always, of course, at liberty to examine each bundle carefully to see that the feathers are of good quality and shape, and properly graded.

There are not many establishments in London where hackles (or fly - dressing materials of any kind) can be procured, but Messrs. Farlow, of 10, Charles Street, St. James's Square, W., Mr. John Forrest, of 24, Thomas Street, Oxford Street, W., and the Army and Navy Stores, may, I think, be relied upon to supply hackles (and materials generally) of good quality.

2. *Coarse-fibred hackles* are obtained from a great variety of birds. As their designation implies, they are opaque feathers, comparatively thick in the fibre, and are as a rule used in their natural colours, though some take the dye fairly well. They usually figure

in that portion of the fly known as the "throat." At times, however, they form the ribbing hackle or the joints (where these are hackles)—*e.g.*, in some grubs.

The accompanying list will be found useful:

> *Partridge.*—Brown from the rump, grey from the breast.
>
> *Grouse.*—From the rump and breast (choose a rather light cock bird).
>
> *Gallina.*—The speckled feathers from the breast, back, and rump (cocks are best). These dye fairly well.
>
> *Woodcock.*—Back and rump.
>
> *Snipe.*—Rump (there are not many of these).
>
> *Landrail.*—Rump and a few of the large wing coverts. These come in useful for patterns of the Spey type.
>
> *Summer Duck* (unbarred) ⎫
> *Teal...* ... ⎪ From the sides (under the wing). There are not
> *Widgeon* ... ⎬ many of these on any one bird. The Summer
> *Pintail* ... ⎭ Duck are dear.
>
> *Golden Pheasant.*—Back and breast. The former are a pale gold colour, the latter a light port wine red.

Cock of the Rock.—Practically all the
feathers can be used as hackles. They
are of a beautiful bright orange colour.

Jay.—The barred blue feathers forming
the middle wing coverts. Not very
many of these will be found to be of
that bright sky blue so much desired,
and from the comparative shortness of
the fibres they are not suitable for large
flies. Jay figures very prominently in
Irish patterns.

All these feathers should be procured from
(male) birds, and, if possible, in their winter
plumage—except Cock of the Rock—January
and February being as a rule the best months.

3. *Special hackles.* These are—

(*a*) The fluffy grey or whitish feathers from
the thigh of a Golden Eagle, and are not, as
may be imagined, particularly easy or cheap
to procure. They are dyed a golden lemon
colour in the Yellow and Avon Eagles.

(*b*) The long-fibred mobile feathers from
the crest and shoulders (black), and the
breast, back, and rump (grey) of the common
Heron.

(*c*) The soft-fibred pseudo-hackles, known

as Spey-cock hackles, from the sides of the
tail of certain domestic fowls. They are of
various colours—viz., metallic bronzy black,
plain brown, freckled brown and cinnamon,
and are rather lacking in translucence, though
very mobile in character. The fibres at the
root of the feather are usually of a different
colour to those of the main body—a greyish-
brown being the commonest tint.

It may be said of hackles in general that
(1) cock's hackles are employed where colour
is the main object; (2) coarse-fibred hackles
serve to keep the ribbing hackle together;*
and (3) special hackles come into requisition
where mobility is the leading feature.

Next in importance to hackles come the
various feathers used for wings. The same
rules affecting the choice of hackles applies
here—*i.e.*, to choose none but feathers from
birds in their best plumage. Unfortunately,
many of these are birds from distant lands,
and one cannot be quite certain whether at the
date of their demise they were or were not in
their best plumage. However, with the exer-

* *E.g.*, in patterns hackled with Heron and Eagle
hackles.

cise of a little discrimination one can usually
tell whether any particular feather is in good
condition or not.   If it has natural gloss, feels
supple to the fingers, and has no fraying or
irregularity at the tips of the fibres, it is probably worth securing.   Care of selection is of
importance when purchasing expensive feathers,
such as Bustard, Peacock, Summer Duck,
Golden Pheasant, and so forth.   There is
nothing more annoying than to have to work
with brittle feathers, especially if a stiff price
has been paid for them.

The easièst and cheapest feathers for winging
to procure are those of some of the duck tribe
—viz., Mallard, Teal, Widgeon, and Pintail.
These may be purchased from the dealers in
bundles of a dozen, but the cheapest way is to
combine two purposes in one, so to speak, by
purchasing the entire bird, selecting the feathers
required, and delivering the carcass to the
guidwife as an item in the house - keeping.
Only male birds, of course, are suitable, and
about the New Year is the best time.   On the
Mallard a few feathers from the saddle only
are of any use.   These are the brown freckled
ones, with. the greyish base to the fibres, which

are used on the plain Mallard wing patterns and on Spey flies.

The Widgeon has good feathers from the saddle (for small patterns) and from the sides under the wings. Teal and Pintail supply feathers under the wings only. All these three last named have feathers very similar to each other in general markings—viz., black stripes on a white background—but a good Teal is the most strongly marked, though the feathers cannot be used as wings for any but small flies. They are very frequently used as throat hackles as well.

Summer Duck (or Canadian Wood-Duck)— the barred feathers—are very expensive items. They are sold for 4s. 6d. per dozen, and each bird has only about a dozen feathers under each wing. Do not buy, or at any rate do not use, Summer Duck feathers until you are fairly proficient at fly-dressing, because they are not very easy to put on and their cost is impressive. The unbarred feathers are cheaper, but they are not often used as wings for salmon flies.*

* Grey Mallard and Egyptian Goose are sometimes used, but the markings are not very strong, and the feathers generally are rather "dead."

For the Dee strip-wing and some of the built-wing patterns the tail feathers of various breeds of Turkey cocks come into requisition. The chief colours are speckled grey, cinnamon, white, black white-tip, and mottled brown (the commonest). The black white-tip is not easy to obtain really good, the white being so often dirty grey instead of pure white. For cinnamon and white I know of no better firm to apply to than Messrs. William Brown, of 54, Union Street, Aberdeen, who also supply fly-tying materials of all sorts and of first-class quality. Turkey tails, capable of producing feathers long enough in the fibre to wing a 3-inch iron are not exactly common, and it is useful to know where such feathers can be got. The mottled brown feather is procurable from the ordinary Christmas Turkey, and need cost nothing. It makes a very pretty strip-wing, is an excellent foundation for the plain upright Mallard wings, and comes in useful for mixed-wings.

The richly-freckled wing and tail feathers of various species of Bustard (including Florican), and the boldly barred black and cinnamon ones from the European species, are invaluable for mixed- and built-wings.   These are expensive, and not often to be had in the best condition, so see to it, when you buy them and pay a long price, that they *are* good.

The strongly marked sepia and cream secondary feathers from a Peacock's wing are also very useful for mixed wings, but they are seldom suitable for winging large patterns, as the fibres are not very long.

White Swan feathers, natural and dyed, are essential for mixed-wings.   The principal colours are red (cardinal for choice), blue (turquoise), lemon yellow, bright orange, and pale grass green.   See that the colours are rich; faded or half tones are not desirable.

The beautifully marked tail feathers of the cock Golden and Amherst Pheasants are extensively used both for built- and mixed-wings.   These fetch a long price, but can usually be procured good.   The centre tail feathers are the ones to secure.   Similarly, the tail feathers of the common Pheasant (cock and hen) come in useful at times for ordinary strip-wings.

Then, of course, Golden Pheasant toppings and neck feathers (commonly known as tippets) are necessary. It is far more satisfactory to buy these in skins, which will cost you anything from 6s. (if you are *very* lucky) to 20s. per skin. Above all, see to it that they are brilliant ; faded toppings and tippets are worse than useless. The toppings should sparkle like champagne when held up to the light, and tippets should be almost red in colour, with the dark bars nearly black by contrast.

For the wings of certain patterns of a large size the bright red sword feathers of the Golden Pheasant are used.*

Other necessary feathers (for " cheeks " and " sides ") supplied in skins are the bright orange breast feathers of the Indian Crow, the golden yellow ones from the breast and throat of the Toucan, the beautiful blue feathers from practically the entire skin of the Blue Chatterer (these should be of the pale electric blue shade, *not* the deep sky-blue, which is much less brilliant), the greenish-blue feathers from the back of the Indian Kingfisher (these are sometimes used as substitutes for Blue

* Sometimes the neck feathers (tippets) and crest feathers (toppings) of this invaluable bird are used as hackles.

Chatterer, as they are cheaper, but they are not so good), the spotted waxy feathers from the neck of the Jungle Cock, and, as already mentioned under hackles, the body feathers from the Cock of the Rock.

The green sword feathers and the bronze moon feathers from the Peacock are also used in connection with wings.

Black Ostrich herl (which can usually be obtained from some fair lady's discarded head-gear) for butts, and Blue and Yellow and Scarlet Macaw tail feathers for horns, complete a fairly workman-like collection of feathers for the amateur fly-dresser.

For bodies a supply of furs, floss silks, Berlin wools, and crewels, must be gathered. Of the natural furs, Grey Squirrel or Silver Monkey, and the fur from a Hare's face, are about the only ones used for salmon flies to any extent, as the dyed Seal's fur is found to be far superior in brilliance to any natural fur, and easier to work with. Silver Monkey is difficult to procure, and the fly-tyer has usually to content himself with Grey Squirrel, which, however, is almost as good. Mohair and Pig's wool have been superseded by the easily dyed and much finer Seal's fur, which can be obtained in all colours. The most useful colours will be found to be bright orange, lemon, fiery brown, scarlet, claret, purple, green, golden olive, dark and light blue, and black. Various pleasing shades can be obtained by an artistic blending of two or more of these " base " colours.

Floss silks are best obtained on reels, and can be procured in some hundreds of different shades from Messrs. Pearsall, who sell about the best on the market. The following are the numbers which, on looking in my box, I find I have been using for the last four years for all manner of flies: 7A, 156A, 160, 41E, 153A, 99, 181, 178, 182, 83.

Floss silk is a most unsatisfactory material in practice and a tiresome substance to work with, as it loses brilliance when wet, gets easily soiled, and has a disgusting habit of discovering the most minute unevenness of surface on the fingers, and becoming in consequence an unsightly and rumpled mess. But so far no good substitute has as yet been discovered. Messrs. Pearsall have recently brought out a vegetable fibre which in brilliance and dye-fast properties imitates floss very well, and in cost is ridiculously cheap; but I found it rather "lumpy" to work with, though in other respects it is much easier to handle than floss. This "fibrone," as it is called, is used by some fly-dressers in mixed-wings. It certainly shows up against the light with remarkable brilliance, and, being rather stiff in consistence, stands out well. But all the same, as a body and tag material it does not possess the smoothness and evenness of floss silk.

Crewels and Berlin wools come in useful for the bodies of certain patterns—*e.g.*, Spey flies, and for butts of others—viz., the Doctors. It is rather surprising that they are not more extensively used for bodies, because they are cheap, easily put on, and can produce most striking effects. A raid on a lady's work-basket will usually furnish enough crewels and Berlin wools of various colours to last a life-time; but in case this suggestion should not meet with the reader's views of honesty, it may be as well to add that a few pence expended in a hosiery emporium will provide for an ample stock of wools of many and various shades.

A supply of tinsels will have to be procured,

and as tinsel of some kind figures in all salmon flies, the fly-dresser will find that this will run into a considerable sum of money. *Tinsels* are supplied in reels either flat, oval, or embossed. Flat tinsels are just fine strips of silver or silver gilt. Oval tinsel consists of a core of floss-silk round which very fine gold or silver wire has been closely bound by machinery. Embossed tinsel is generally silver, and, as its name indicates, is just embossed flat silver tinsel. Gold and silver *threads* are made on a similar principle, but these are round instead of oval in section. Two or more strands of thread twisted together like the strands of an ordinary hempen rope constitute what is known as *twist.*

About eight different thicknesses of gold and silver, flat, and oval tinsels will be required. Many people dispense entirely with the finer sizes of flat tinsel, and employ the oval instead. About three sizes of embossed silver tinsel and twist will also be required.

This pretty well exhausts the list of materials that any reasonable amateur need wish to collect, but other necessary requirements will be tying silks and wax. For tying on the gut loop a fairly stout silk may (in the large flies) be employed, and for this the natural undyed silk is by far the best. I use a silk supplied by Messrs. William Whiteley, Ltd., on reels containing 200 yards, and specified as " cream No. 178." It is quite cheap and very strong, and comes in useful for all manner of purposes, such as tying hooks to gut, mending breakages, and so forth. It can be unravelled into three separate strands, and thus be employed for varying purposes, according to expediency or choice.

For actual fly-dressing Pearsall's gossamer is the best. This is also supplied on reels in a variety of colours. For salmon flies the colour of the tying silk does not matter much, unless one is very particular; but as I find that the bright orange is the strongest, that is the colour I generally use.

As to wax, the ordinary cobbler's is, I think, the best. Again, if one is very particular, some flies may appear to require their tying silk treated with so-called colourless wax. This never grips so well as the cobbler's wax, and deteriorates rather quickly. Either kind of wax should preferably be kept in pieces about the size of peas in water.

Varnish, of course, must not be forgotten, and for salmon flies I do not think there is anything to surpass the black varnish sold by dealers for the purpose. The ordinary shellac will do, and it has the merit of drying quickly ; but for permanency the black varnish is much to be preferred. Once allowed to dry and harden properly, the head of a fly treated with it will outlast the gut loop and the feathers themselves.

Perhaps a few words may be added on the subject of storing materials.

Each individual will, of course, arrange his feathers, furs, etc., according to his own particular ideas, bearing in mind, however, the fundamental importance of so disposing them that they will be (1) protected from the ravages of moth, light, and impure air ; (2) readily accessible at all times ; and (3) free from unnecessary bulk, so as to admit of their carriage from place to place without much trouble or the monopolization of an unduly large amount of room.

Undoubtedly the best receptacle for keeping fly-dressing materials is a cabinet with drawers of varying sizes, some of which are provided with divisions for keeping certain articles separate. I have recently had such a cabinet made. It will hold every requirement, including hooks and implements, and yet is of portable dimensions. Hackles and feathers for wings are kept in separate envelopes in one of the drawers arranged on the card file index principle. Skins and wings are kept in a separate drawer, and seal's fur, floss, tinsels, wools, etc., and hooks, are also kept separate, in their respective partitions, in two additional drawers with which this cabinet is supplied. The drawers themselves are made of cedar wood, which is an excellent preventive against moth. The outside of the cabinet is made of mahogany, which insures strength and a capacity to stand some knocking about. It is provided with a sliding door, which can be locked, the purpose of which is to keep the drawers from falling out, and their contents out of the reach of interference at the hands of unauthorized individuals. The whole cabinet, the outside dimensions of which are only $14\frac{1}{2}$ inches by 12 inches by $12\frac{1}{2}$ inches, is contained in a stout canvas cover, provided with a leather strap, in which it is carried when travelling.

CHAPTER V

THE fly-tyer will find certain tools necessary to help him in his work.

The bare necessities will probably be covered by a pair of scissors, a pair of hackle pliers, and a darning needle. But I prefer a rather more elaborate armoury, and can testify to the enormous advantage in having a well-selected assortment of good implements, both as regards the quality of the flies turned out and the speed with which they can be dressed.

At least three pairs of good scissors will be required: (1) an ordinary short-bladed pair of nail scissors for cutting gut and tinsel; (2) a fine curved pair, commonly known as cuticle scissors by manicures, for cutting off close the various materials employed in the bodies of flies; and (3) a fine straight-pointed pair as

used for embroidery work, to finish off neatly
the waste ends of wings after they have been
tied on (and for other close work).   It is unnecessary to point out that all scissors should

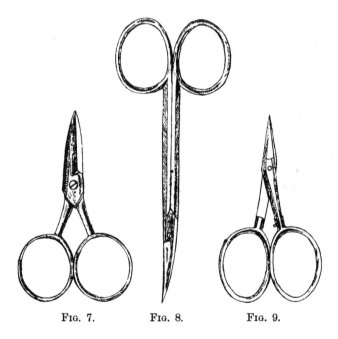

FIG. 7.   FIG. 8.   FIG. 9.

be very sharp, and *kept* sharp and clean (see
Figs. 7, 8, and 9).

Of hackle pliers at least three different kinds
will be found advisable : (1) a small pair for
small hackles ; (2) a big pair for large hackles ;

and (3) a pair with a serrated grip for stout
tinsels.   The last kind is not usually sold by
tackle dealers.   I had mine made by a surgical
instrument maker, who charged me a shilling
per pair.   No doubt any surgical instrument
maker will be only too glad to make them at

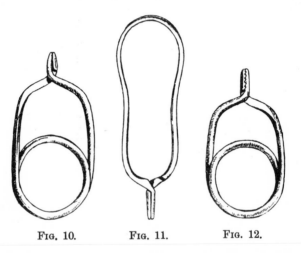

FIG. 10.   FIG. 11.   FIG. 12.

the same price.   It cannot be too strongly
urged that the less one handles tinsel with the
bare fingers the better for the tinsel, and these
pliers will be found invaluable for gripping
both flat and oval tinsel firmly, enabling one
to wind it tightly round the body of the fly
(see Figs. 10, 11, and 12).

It is an advantage to have several pairs of spare pliers.   They come in useful for holding tinsels, hackles, and small feathers, when these are being sorted before the dressing of a fly

FIG. 13.

begins, and where sudden draughts are liable to occur.

A pair of stout dissecting forceps (Fig. 13) and a fine pair (Fig. 14) (as used by bacteriologists and oculists) will be found almost a necessity for picking up various small articles

FIG. 14.

from the table, or selecting hackles easily and quickly from a pile.

A sharp knife will be needed for paring away the loose ends of the gut forming the loop, or preparing a Jay's hackle, and for a variety of other purposes.

A stiletto (Fig. 15), or an ordinary stout darning needle (for picking out fur, separating feathers, etc.), completes a list of tools which will be found useful.

The question of a vice now arises.

Some divergence of opinion exists as to the necessity of a vice for salmon fly-tying. Professional tyers usually dispense entirely with it on the grounds that they have far more complete command of the fly in all its stages, and can see better what they are doing when they

FIG. 15.

rely upon their fingers alone. Personally I do not think a vice at all necessary for salmon flies. Tying without it certainly puts you in a position of far greater independence. You can dress a fly in almost any position—sitting, standing, or even reclining. It will probably not frequently be necessary to assume gymnastic and uncomfortable attitudes when the desire to dress a fly arises, but the practical point will come in at some primitive inn or fishing hut, where the accommodation is not

good and the light at a bad angle. With a
vice you need a table, in the first place; and
secondly, the light must fall at a certain angle.
Very often when away from home a convenient
light (especially artificial) is not available.   It
is then a great advantage to be able to dispense with the table, and (like Mahomet and
the mountain) to go to the light and adjust
your own person to the proper angle, when it
is impossible to make the light come to you
and adjust *it* to the proper angle.   I have ere
now had to stand actually under an artificial
light before I could get enough to see what I
was doing, and if I had been unable to dispense with a vice I should have had to dispense
with the fly until the following morning, when
probably I should want to be fishing and not
dressing flies.

Even when a good table and a good light
are available, tying with a vice, implying as
it does that the hook has to remain fixed in
one position all the time, is much more of a
strain upon the eyes than using the unaided
hands.

Nevertheless, a vice has its advantages.

For instance, when tying floss silk bodies in

hot weather, a vice makes it easier to avoid soiling the delicate silk with the fingers. Again, in the case of flies that need a lot of " tying in " at the tail end, where the number of things—*e.g.*, two or three kinds of tinsel, a ribbing hackle and body material (as in the Spey flies)—are somewhat cumbersome to con trol, a vice is a distinct help ; and in the case of small double hooks, and of very long-shanked hooks, the strain of holding with the forefinger and thumb of the left hand is considerable, and a vice is undoubtedly a relief.

But, for all that, I do not think a vice is an absolute necessity ; and so far as concerns the tying of wings of whatsoever variety, I believe that the unaided fingers always lead to better results.

If asked to express my own opinion, I should say borrow ; or, if you must and can conveniently afford it, buy a vice, and *learn* to tie flies with it. But having once acquired familiarity with the necessary manipulations, dispense with it ; and if you have bought it, only use it on those occasions — some of which I have mentioned above—where its

use really presents advantages over the unaided fingers.* †

* A vice will cost anything from 5s. to 35s. If it is
decided only to *learn* to tie with a vice, and one cannot be
borrowed, it is hardly necessary to pay a long price for
one, and therefore I should not recommend an expensive
one.   But the truth of the saying "cheap and nasty"
must not be lost sight of, and it will probably be found
that the expenditure of a reasonable sum will lead to more
satisfactory results than what at the time appeared to be
a bargain.   Messrs. Holtzappel, in the Haymarket, sell an
excellent vice at 35s., which will last a lifetime; but there
are many useful patterns at a cheaper figure which will in
all likelihood answer every reasonable requirement.

† In the lessons that follow the various manipulations
are described as though the fingers alone, unaided by a vice,
were being employed.   The descriptions, however, will
apply, with the necessary and obvious adaptations, equally
well if a vice is used, except in the first lesson, where, in
point of fact, more satisfactory results are always achieved
without a vice.

CHAPTER VI

PREPARATIONS

BEFORE starting to dress a fly it is rather important to make your dispositions so that the maximum of comfort in working is secured, and therefore the best results are insured.

It is, of course, of prime importance to have a good light. A room with a window facing north is best, and the light should be so disposed that it falls over the left shoulder.

In the matter of furniture, a solid deal table with roomy drawers at the sides, and with a plain unvarnished top which can be scrubbed easily, is to be preferred to any. A kitchen table is just the thing.

For seating accommodation, a bench running along the whole length of the table is more convenient than a chair.

If you are likely to be using the same table and seat for any length of time, it will be advisable to dispose your implements and materials around you in a certain definite and regular order, so that you can almost with your eyes shut put your hand on the particular article required, and not have to fumble in several places before securing it.

A white background is always best to work upon, and if you cannot obtain the use of a white deal-topped table, a white cloth or a piece of white cardboard should be employed, as you will then obviate the waste of many valuable minutes in the search for such elusive things as small hooks pieces of fine tinsel and waxed silk—a proceeding which spoils temper as well as wastes time.

When possible, it is of course far better to work by daylight. But very often the necessity will arise to dress flies by artificial light. The best artificial light is, without a doubt, a powerful hanging electric lamp, provided with a reflecting shade, to throw the light downwards and adjustable to any distance to suit individual requirements. When using the unaided fingers the light is best adjusted so as to be immediately above the hands. If a vice is used, the light should be a little to the left of, and only a few inches away from, the fly being dressed ; but, of course, in every case it should be shaded from the eyes. It will be found, however, that under any circumstances the use of a vice with an artificial light is rather trying.

A white linen apron—though it may look ridiculous—is a great convenience. Coarse linen, by the way, is an excellent material on which to wipe the fingers clean from such sticky substances as wax and varnish. An apron, forming as it does a lap, is extremely useful for intercepting various small articles that seem to have an irresistible attraction for the floor, and frequently elude the grasp of the fingers. People who—like myself—have spent many heated minutes searching for a hook, a small feather, or a hackle pliers which has dropped on to the carpet, will not be disposed to belittle the importance of the linen apron in this capacity of "long-stop." (Hackle pliers are particularly irritating things to drop on to a carpet—they bounce so.)

A saucer in which is a piece of cotton-wool soaked in methylated spirit will be necessary for the cleansing of the fingers from wax. (In dressing a fly it is most important to have the fingers always clean.)

Unless you happen to be on terms of the happiest and completest understanding with the ruling spirit of the domestic establishment, it is advisable to provide yourself with a waste-paper basket, which you will keep close beside you, and into which you will carefully put all bits and loose ends, so as to prevent an indignant outcry the following morning when the waste products of fly-dressing have to be disposed of. I must confess that the domestic who has to sweep up pieces of unravelled and clinging floss silk from a sticky pile carpet has my profound sympathy. Nevertheless, I am afraid I must frequently be the cause of black and evil thoughts in a fellow-creature for the reason that, though I always take the precaution of having a waste-paper basket close at hand, I somehow almost invariably forget its existence, and in consequence allow the bulk of my fly-dressing *detritus* to fall on to the carpet, from which it has to be removed —but not by me—at the expense of much energy and vexation of the spirit.

Whatever you do, do not allow a bare hook —especially a double hook—to remain on the carpet. The consequences may exceed the limits of an ordinary joke, especially if there are dogs and children about.

It is inadvisable to smoke when engaged in the serious occupation of dressing a fly. If you smoke a pipe, it will constantly be going out, and you will consume many matches and develop a throat. If you smoke a cigarette, you will put it aside to smoke by itself, and probably burn the house down, or do some other damage.

To begin with, you will probably have many mishaps, such as broken silks, feathers that refuse to lie properly, hackles that come undone or destroy themselves at critical moments, etc. Most men resort to swearing at such a time. This is not a remedy, though it may relieve the feelings.

I am afraid, however, I cannot with an easy conscience express disapproval of such exhibitions of feeling, neither do I feel it appropriate to urge the cultivation of a serene patience. From practical experience, however, I can say that this stage, which, like mumps, is painful while it lasts, is not dangerous, and will in time cure itself and leave no apparent ill effects.

CHAPTER VII

THE FIRST LESSON—THE GUT LOOP

WE are now really ready to begin the creation of a salmon fly, and our first lesson will have to be very carefully learnt, for upon the soundness and general good quality of this the first stage of our task will depend not only the symmetrical appearance of the fly, but its durability in practice.

Take a hook (say a "rational" 1½ inches long, see Plate X., Group C) and proceed to test it so as to be quite sure that it is a good one. Examine the point and barb carefully. The former must be very sharp, and the latter should not be deeply cut. Fix the point into the edge of the table, or into any piece of soft wood, and holding it by the tip of the shank, give a sudden smart pull so as to make the bend gape widely. After this test the hook should spring back to its original shape, and you can then safely pronounce it sound. Except in the smallest sizes, it should not be possible actually to break a hook when subjecting it to this test.

Having satisfied yourself as to these requirements, it will be well to study the free end of the shank to see that it tapers off evenly and roundly. If it has not been so made by the hook manufacturers, it should be done by yourself with the aid of a keen file. This may appear at first sight a rather needless refinement, but I can assure the reader that it enormously facilitates the production of a neat small head to the fly (an undoubted advantage practically, and a hall-mark of a high-class work), and I am inclined to think that it achieves a sound mechanical principle by making the transition between the soft pliable gut to the hard rigid steel as gradual as possible.

It should be an invariable rule with the fly-dresser to examine, test, and prepare a hook, as indicated in the two preceding paragraphs, before beginning any work upon it.

Having thus carefully selected the hook, choose a piece of twisted gut of a thickness proportionate to the size and weight of the hook. Lay this along the shank of the hook so that one end of it is on that portion of the hook where the straightness of the shank begins to merge into the curve of the bend. (This is an important landmark to bear in mind in

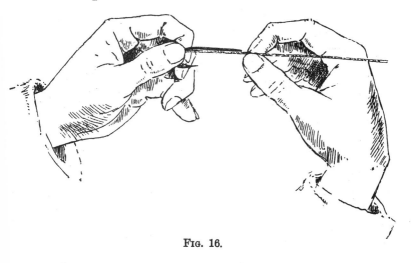

Fig. 16.

subsequent operations.) Holding it thus with the forefinger and thumb of the left hand, make a nick in it with the right thumbnail at a point about $\frac{1}{8}$ inch beyond the extremity of the free end of the shank (Fig. 16). Double it over, and cut off when the doubled portion coincides with the end held by the left fore-

finger and thumb. Now, with the forefingers
and thumbs of both hands, twist the nicked
portion tightly for about $\frac{1}{8}$ inch on either side
of the nick. Grasping the looped end firmly
with the nails of the left forefinger and thumb,

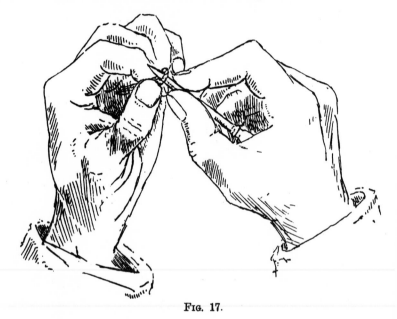

Fig. 17.

pass it over the point of a stiletto, so that a
rounded loop of the required size is formed
(Fig. 17). By working the stiletto from side
to side and pinching the gut more and more
tightly with the nails of the left forefinger and

thumb, a sort of "neck" is produced, where the twist of the gut is straightened out and a nice round loop of tightly twisted gut is formed. The size of the loop will, of course, depend upon the size of the fly, but only experience will teach what the size should be.   It is a generally accepted maxim that the loop should be as small as possible, within reasonable limits.

Before laying it on to the hook, the twisted gut should have been manipulated into the

FIG. 18.

shape indicated in Fig. 18.   The next thing is to wax a piece of silk.

Unwind about a foot of the natural silk mentioned on p. 73 from its reel.   Between the tips of the right forefinger and thumb work a piece of cobbler's wax about the size of a small pea, until it begins to get soft.   Press it flat, and then pass the silk through from end to end quickly but steadily *once* (see Figs. 19 and 20).   To an expert once will be quite enough, and the silk will have been evenly and lightly waxed, but in such a way that it will "bite" well.

The same manipulation will be required for the fine " dressing " silk.

To wax silk well is not easy. It requires practice, and the fingers must be at a certain

Fig. 19.

temperature so as to soften the wax to the desirable consistency. The beginner will probably break the silk frequently, and have it waxed heavily in lumps instead of lightly and

uniformly. The secrets are to have the wax
properly softened, to press it flat between the
fingers, and to draw it steadily and quickly
through without a pause. It is inadvisable to
wax long lengths of silk—18 inches is about as

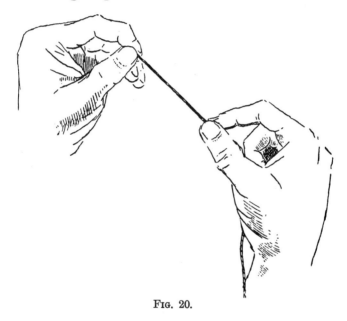

FIG. 20.

long as is necessary or practicable—and it is a
good plan, while you are about it, to wax
several lengths at the same time to serve for
tying the same fly throughout, and so avoid
the necessity of waxing fresh pieces in the

middle of the dressing. There are other methods of waxing silk, but after trying most of them, I have come to the conclusion that the method indicated is the most satisfactory from every point of view.

After waxing a sufficient quantity of silk, the wax must be got rid of from the fingers. You will have to do this as best you can. It clings on some fingers and on certain days more tenaciously than on others. There is, however, always the saucer with the piece of cotton-wool soaked in methylated spirit at hand, and this, together with the linen apron or a duster, will enable the fingers to be thoroughly cleansed of all adherent wax. It is most important to keep the fingers always quite clean.

Now take the hook in the left hand, and holding it bend upwards, make a few wide spiral turns with the waxed silk on the shank towards the head up to about $\frac{1}{8}$ inch from the end. Lay the doubled twisted gut upon the shank so that the neck of the loop already referred to exactly coincides with the tip of the shank and the plane of the loop is at right angles to the plane of the bend of the hook (Fig. 21).

Fix the gut to the shank, beginning at the point where the spiral coils of silk on the bare shank left off, with tight, close, even turns of silk towards the bend, leaving about ⅛ inch of

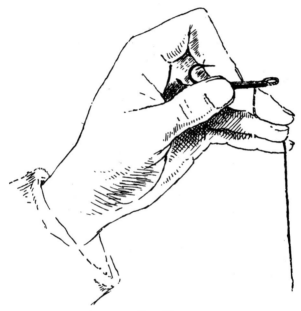

FIG. 21.

the shank at the head exposed (Fig. 22). This uncovered portion of the shank will eventually be occupied by the throat and head of the fly, and it is important to have clean ground to work on there for that purpose. The coils of

silk here, and with few exceptions throughout
the dressing of a fly, are in the natural direc-

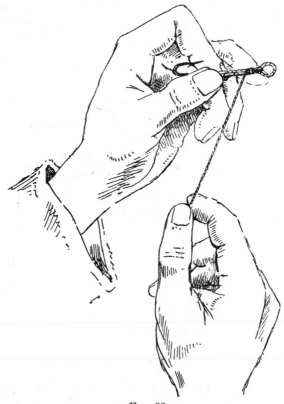

Fig. 22.

tion — *i.e.*, over the shank and away from you,
mechanically referred to as clockwise.

Continue winding tailwards, taking care all

the time to keep the twisted gut straight along
the shank, until the middle of the shank is
reached.   At this point you begin to taper the
twisted gut.   This is an operation requiring
some delicacy, and is only to be attempted
with a very sharp, strong knife.   It is done

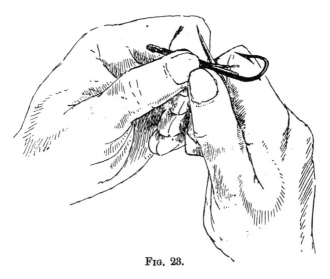

Fig. 23.

by very gradually paring away each piece of
twisted gut separately at the sides (Fig. 23) in
such a way that just previous to where the
shank of the hook merges into the bend the
two pieces of gut coincide to form a point.
Even in experienced hands this operation is

not always performed with complete success, so the beginner must not be discouraged if his efforts seem to fall very short of the results implied as necessary from these written words.

The importance of a perfect taper arises in the case of tinsel bodies. It does not possess such significance in fur or even floss bodies, where intelligent padding will as a rule obliterate any faultiness of tapering in the tying of the gut loop. But its importance in tinsel bodies cannot be too strongly emphasized, for in this case padding will seldom rectify the defect, especially as most tinsel bodies are required to be dressed thin; and therefore, as it is necessary to acquire proficiency in accurate tapering, and as accurate tapering is a sound principle to keep before one, and as sound principles are for their own sake desirable to follow, I recommend the reader to tie all his gut loops as though his intention was in every case to make a tinsel-bodied fly. Thus will be ingrained a good habit and a natural tendency towards thoroughly sound work, which are not only desirable in themselves, but will in the long run prove most economical of time and trouble.

There are two other methods whereby a correct taper may be secured. The first is to cut each end of the doubled, twisted gut before laying it on the hook with a straight-bladed, strong, sharp pair of scissors. The second is to soak the gut thoroughly in warm water, and allow the ends to unravel and straighten before tying on. The unravelled and straightened ends can then be very easily pared down, but this method is open to the objection that the gut will, when dry, shrink, and so possibly loosen the security of its attachment ; and the gut loop so treated has a disagreeable tendency to twist round and depart from its proper relation to the hook, with the likelihood added that the working of the fly will be impaired.

On the whole, I think that the method of tapering first mentioned, though not the easiest, is the best ultimately.*

Whatever method of tapering is adopted, the thing to bear in mind is that the extremity of the gut should reach a point slightly in front of the part of the hook eventually to be occupied by the butt, if there is one, or the

* Loosely twisted gut is much easier to taper than tightly twisted gut.

hindmost portion of the body in any case. Many expert fly-dressers say that there should be a considerable interval occupied by the hook-shank alone, so as to allow room for the materials to be tied in at the posterior portion of the body ; but I am inclined to think, after many trials, that this is not the easiest way of securing a symmetrical taper.

Having tapered the twisted gut with the knife, continue the tying silk in close, tight,

Fig. 24.

even coils tailwards, until the gut has been entirely covered (see Fig. 24).

When smoothness of body is particularly desired, it is a good plan to hold the hook close to a fire, so as to soften the wax, and then vigorously to rub the portion occupied by the waxed silk up and down with a stiletto.

The hook is now ready to take the dressing of the fly.

CHAPTER VIII

THE SECOND LESSON—A WINGLESS PATTERN
OR GRUB

THIS is a very simple pattern, without wings, tag, butt, or tail, and will be a useful one for the beginner to start operations on.

The first thing to do is to fix the stout binding silk with the fine dressing silk. Do this by letting the former hang downwards—having first given it a firm pull to insure the close and even set of the preceding coils—and catch it with the tying silk in the manner indicated in Fig. 25 and (magnified) in Fig. 26. Take two or three close tight turns tailwards with the dressing silk, and cut off close the free end of the binding silk and the shorter end of the dressing silk.

This manipulation is applicable for tying in any loose ends of silk, and comes in useful when it is necessary to continue with a fresh

103

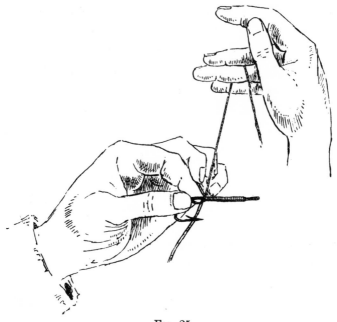

Fig. 25.

Fig. 26.

piece of silk, or when, as will often happen
at first, the silk breaks.

Now take a length of broad, oval silver
tinsel, and laying it under the hook-shank,
attach it with two turns of silk tailwards
(Fig. 27).   Unravel a portion of the free end

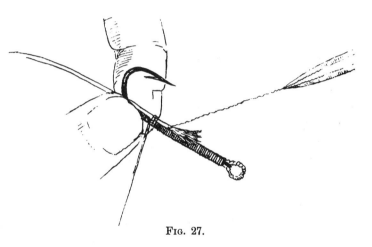

FIG. 27.

lying against the shank of the hook, and cut
off the floss core thus exposed on a slant with
the curved-bladed scissors.   This will help the
taper of the body.

Choose a good cock's hackle of a suitable
size, bearing in mind the points to observe as
regards cock's hackles generally as indicated

on a previous page (Fig. 28), and proceed to prepare it for laying on.* This process is called " doubling" a hackle, and is illustrated in Figs. 29 and 30, which, I think, speak for themselves. In doubling always hold the best (*i.e.*, the outer) surface towards· you, and press the opposite fibres, so that their inner or dullest surfaces are opposed to each other. Lay the forefinger of the left hand first on the " left " fibres, and then use the thumb to

Fig. 28.

pinch the fibres of both sides to the right and downwards with a semicircular movement. Treat short lengths of the hackle in this way in sections, and do not attempt to do it all in one movement. A moistened left forefinger and thumb will considerably facilitate the pro-

* The hackle figured is a furnace, but any kind of cock's hackle will do for the purpose at this stage.

cess.   A properly doubled hackle should have
the appearance indicated in Fig. 31.

Now lay the tip of the hackle with the

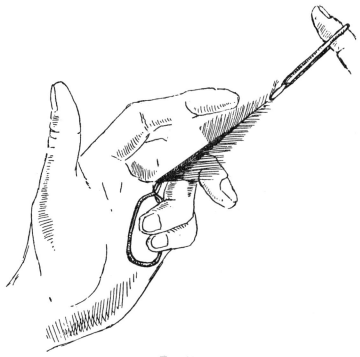

FIG. 29.

fibres pointing to the left and downwards on
the side of the hook nearest to you at the
point where the last coils of the dressing silk
ended, and fix with a few turns tailwards.

E

The next stage is the formation of the body.
Take some dyed Seal's fur (say scarlet),

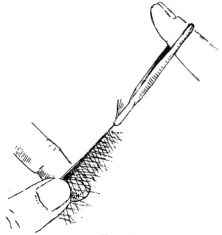

FIG. 30.

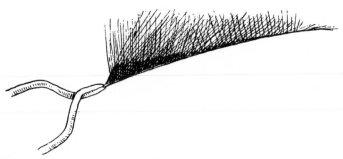

FIG. 31.

break it up a little in the fingers, and spin
it lightly into the form of a spindle. Lay

one end of this spindle on the side of the hook farthest from you, exactly over the last coil of silk ; put it " in stop " by holding it against the hook with the middle finger of the left hand, and then spin it on to the dressing silk by twisting the latter from left to right—*i.e.*, in the same direction as that in which you would wind an ordinary keyless watch. If the silk has been properly waxed, the fur should adhere firmly ; but it is important to prevent the silk from untwisting by keeping a firm hold on it with the right forefinger and thumb, and stretching it fairly tightly at the same time (see Fig. 32, in which the left middle finger is holding the dressing silk with the fur spun on to it " in stop ").

Wind the fur in open, but firmly and evenly applied turns towards the head up to the point where the bare hook-shank appears. Hitch the silk (having pressed back any surplus fur adhering) in between the hook-shank and the gut loop. Now grip the free end of the tinsel with the serrated pliers, and wind it tightly in even, open coils towards the head up to where the fur ends ; hold it " in stop," pull it tight downwards and towards

you with the right hand, and fix it with two
turns of silk towards the head and then with
two turns towards the tail immediately over
these (Fig. 33). Cut off the loose end of the
tinsel, leaving about $\frac{1}{8}$ inch free ; unravel this

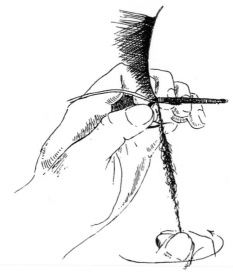

Fig. 32.

free end, and cut off closely on a slant. The
free ends of all oval tinsels, twists, and threads
should be made to lie absolutely under the
shank of the hook, so as to occupy the groove
formed by the gut loop. This is done at the

time when the tinsel is being pulled tight, and tied in, as just previously described, by pressing it backwards with the right thumb-nail at the point where it is tied under the shank with the second headward turn of the silk, and then bringing the free end forwards, so as to lie under and in a straight line with the

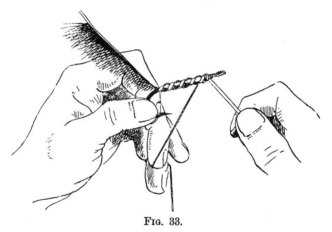

Fig. 33.

shank.   This is really rather an important precaution to adopt, as it greatly helps in the making of a neat smooth head, which, as I have already indicated, is a hall-mark of good work.

The hackle must now be wound round the body.

FIG. 34.

Hitch the silk between gut loop and hook as before (see Fig. 34), grip the hackle by the end of the stem

with the ordinary hackle pliers, and wind the hackle round, keeping the stem immediately

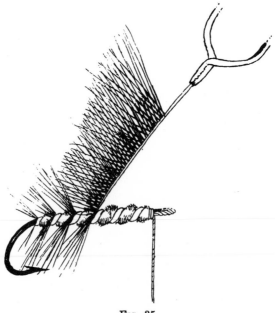

FIG. 35.

behind and close up to each coil of the ribbing tinsel, and the doubled fibres pointing back-

wards all the time (see Fig. 35).   After each
turn the fibres should be smoothed backwards
with the right forefinger and thumb, the
hackle being held "in stop" by the left
middle finger in the meanwhile.

Continue winding in this way towards the

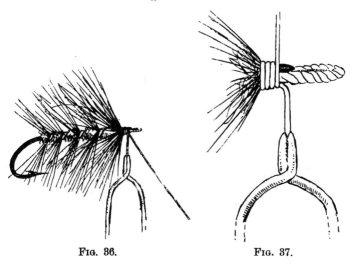

FIG. 36.   FIG. 37.

head until the turns reach the point where the
ribbing tinsel ends, then unhitch the silk and
wind it closely from the last previous coil
towards the head until only just sufficient of
the bare shank of the hook is exposed as will
suffice to form the head, and wind the hackle
closely and evenly over these turns of silk up

to where they end. Strip off any superfluous
fibres (if any), and tie in the bare stem in the
same way as indicated for the ribbing tinsel

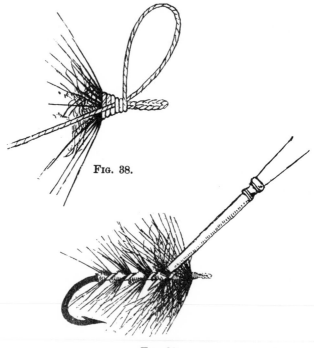

Fig. 38.

Fig. 39.

(Figs. 36 and 37). Cut off the stem closely
on a slant, and over it apply the whip finish to
the silk (Fig. 38). Cut off and smooth the
silk by drawing the back of the right thumb-

nail firmly all round the head in a series of semicircular movements, beginning close to the gut loop, and ending at the roots of the hackle.

Pick out the fur with a stiletto (Fig. 39), apply a little varnish to the head, and the fly is now complete.

CHAPTER IX

THE THIRD LESSON—A SIMPLE STRIP-WINGED
PATTERN, WITH A PLAIN FUR BODY:
(*a*) WINGS UPRIGHT; (*b*) WINGS SLOPING
(*e.g.*, MARCH BROWN)

THIS is in many respects an important lesson,
the manipulations involved being a sort of
skeleton of practically all those required in
dressing the great majority of patterns in
general use. When the reader has mastered
the details of this lesson, he may venture
to attempt the creation of the more elaborate
patterns with some degree of confidence, and
accordingly the time and trouble spent over it
will be well repaid.

It will be advisable in this and in all subsequent dressings to collect and, if necessary,
prepare beforehand all the materials required,
so as to have them within reach, and avoid
delay in searching for any item during the
course of dressing. It is a sound principle to

dress every fly, up to the winging stage at all
events, in one continuous process, without a
stop or interval; and therefore it is necessary
to have each component part ready to tie in
at once, without even having to put the hook
down.

The materials required here will be—

    (1) Fine flat silver tinsel for the tag.

    (2) Broader flat tinsel for the ribbing.

    (3) Unbarred Summer Duck feathers, strands of which are used for the tail.

    (4) The pelt from a Hare's face to form the body.

    (5) The long-fibred brown freckled feathers from the rump of the common Partridge for the throat.

    (6) The centre feather, or two feathers, each from the opposite sides of a hen Pheasant's tail, strips of which are tied in as wings.

You will require about 2 inches of both
(1) and (2). Polish both by gripping one
extremity in the stout dissecting forceps,
and then drawing firmly through a piece of

chamois-leather two or three times. Cut off
a wedge-shaped piece from one extremity
of (2), as shown in Fig. 40.

Strip off from the centre quill fibres from
opposite sides of (3). If this is done with
a quick firm movement of the hands, a small
portion of the flue should remain attached,
which will keep the fibres more or less together. Place the opposite strips of fibres
one over the other, back to back, pinch their

FIG. 40.

bases together, and, following their natural
curve, smooth them out flat against each other.

Tear off small tufts of (4) with the dissecting forceps. Tease the fur out lightly,
and with the right forefinger work it into the
shape of a loose spindle in the groove formed
by raising the fingers of the left hand upwards
at right angles to the palm.

Select a good hackle from (5), and having
removed the fluff at the base, prepare it as you
would a cock's hackle (as described in the previous chapter).

Take the hook—a 1½-inch iron (with the gut loop attached, and the fine waxed dressing silk tied in, of course)—in the left forefinger and thumb as before, and tie in (1) as shown in Fig. 41.   One firm turn of the silk is sufficient, and by lapping it afterwards in open turns over the shank towards the head, and hitching it between the shank and gut loop,

Fig. 41.

the free end will be conveniently out of the way.   Now, gripping the free end of (1) with the ordinary hackle pliers, wind it tightly in close even coils to the left until you have reached a point almost exactly above the extremity of the barb (Fig. 42).   At this point begin winding back to the right over the previous coils.   When these latter have been completely covered, unwind the dressing silk up to and *including* the coil which tied in the tinsel. Take one more turn of (1), and tie it in firmly with three or four turns of silk towards the left (Fig. 43). These turns should be immediately to the left, and, as it were, in

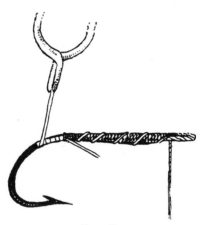

FIG. 42.

continuation of those wound round the hook before the tinsel was laid on The last of these coils of silk should mark the hindmost extremity of the body, which in most hooks will occupy a position immediately above the point where the barb begins.

From what I can gather, this method of

tying a plain tinsel tag is not generally known.
I think it is an easier, quicker, and neater
method than the others known to me.   To
my mind, for plain tinsel tags, flat tinsel is
infinitely to be preferred to oval tinsel or
twist.

The waste ends of the tinsel should each

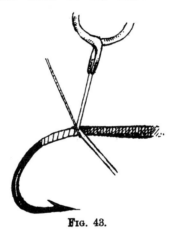

Fig. 43.

be cut off on a slant, so as to meet at a
common point on the upper surface of the
shank.

Take the Summer Duck feathers which
have been prepared for the tail (3), and lay
them on the hook with their natural curve
pointing upwards, as in Fig. 44, exercising

your judgment as to what you consider to be
the proper length for the tail.

Throw a loose turn of silk over, and having
grasped the fibres to the left of, and close up
to, this turn of silk with the left forefinger and
thumb, hold the silk "in catch," and pull it

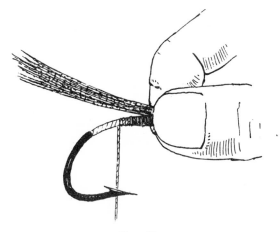

Fig. 44.

gradually tight. (See Fig. 45, which illustrates
the little and ring fingers of the left hand
holding the silk "in catch.") It is important
to keep the apposed strips on edge—*i.e.*, in a
vertical plane—throughout the whole manipulation, so that the natural curve is not displaced, and the tail is made to "sit" nicely.

This can be done by keeping the forefinger and thumb of both hands touching each other whilst the silk is being drawn tight.   (In the

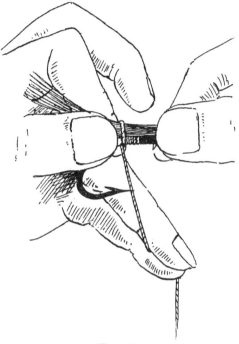

Fig. 45.

diagram the fingers and thumbs are shown wide apart, in order not to obscure the point it is intended to illustrate.)

Still holding the silk tightly " in catch," shift

the grip of the left forefinger and thumb forward, so as to grasp the point where it ties in the tail; hold it "in stop," at the same time releasing it from "catch," and take three more turns over the fibres towards the head of the fly. Hold "in catch," and release from "stop."

If the silk has been well waxed, four turns as described will be sufficient to keep the tail firm, and the ribbing tinsel (2) can now be tied in.

Still holding the silk "in catch," place the tapered end of the tinsel on the side of the hook nearest to you (with the cut edge looking upwards), and keeping the tinsel in that position by including it within the grip of the left thumb upon the hook, release the silk from "catch," and wind it tightly and evenly to the left over the tinsel and over the coils which have tied in the tail and the waste ends of the tag respectively, down to the point where the tag begins.

Cut off the waste ends of the root of the tail on a slant (Fig. 46).*

* The illustration shows two turns of silk only and a space for a third and a fourth turn before the beginning of the tag. That is to say, four turns of silk to the left

Now spin the fur on to the silk and form
the body.   This and the two following stages
—viz., winding the ribbing and tying the
throat—differ in no material degree from the
corresponding stages described in the preceding lesson, and the details therefore will
be omitted.   The ribbing tinsel, however,

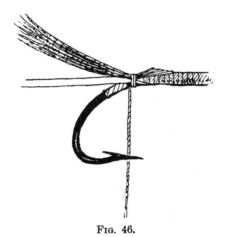

FIG. 46.

being flat, may be cut off close without the
manipulation necessary for oval tinsel.   Always

have sufficed to tie in the free ends of the tag, four turns
to the right to tie the tail, and two turns to the left to tie
in the ribbing, leaving a space to be occupied by an
additional turn of silk over the tinsel and by the first
turn of the fur-dubbed silk for the body.

remember to wind firmly and to pull tight before finishing off.

At this stage the fly should have the appearance shown in Fig. 47.

The wings must now be put on.

Cut off with a sharp knife a " left " and a " right ' strip from the hen Pheasant's tail (6)

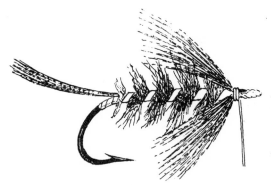

Fig. 47.

with a portion of the centre quill adhering to each (Fig. 48), and see that they match each other in breadth, length, and markings.

In strip-wing patterns, it is most important that the opposite strips should be of the same length, otherwise it would be impossible to get that symmetrical " set " which, so necessary in all types of wings generally, is par-

ticularly so in this one. That is why it is
an advantage always to take the strips from
the opposite sides of the central tail feathers.
A further point to bear in mind—and a very
important one in strip-winged flies generally—
is that the strips should be of a length propor-

Fig. 48.

tionate to the size of the hook being dressed.
For instance, the " set " of strips which are
disproportionately long for the size of the hook
is not attractive to the eye, as the natural
curve of the fibres is lost. Apart from this,
and because they have to be tied in some distance from their bases, they disintegrate very

easily, and are therefore more troublesome to use. This is especially evident in the case of Mallard strips. Generally speaking, the nearer to their bases—*i.e.*, to the piece of quill left adhering—strips can be tied in on to the hook, the better will it be in every way.

Now, there are four separate styles of strip-winging, and two different methods of manipulation are involved.

Strip-wings may be tied in so as to lie entirely on the top of the shank—*i.e.*, with a vertical inclination—or they may be tied so as to encircle the shank partly—*i.e.*, with a sloping or horizontal inclination. In each case "right" and "left" strips may form either the right and left wings or the left and right wings respectively. Or to put it concisely—

(i.) Wings tied vertically—(*a*) each wing of a strip from the corresponding side of the feather; (*b*) each wing of a strip from the opposite side of the feather.

(ii.) Wings tied horizontally — (*a*) each wing of a strip from the corresponding side of the feather; (*b*) each wing of a strip from the opposite side of the feather.

(i.) and (ii.) involve two separate and distinct methods of manipulation, which together produce the four different styles—(i.), (*a*) and (*b*), and (ii.), (*a*) and (*b*) (see Plate XII.).

(i.) In this method both wings are tied on together at the same time, and, as is the case with all wings which are dressed in this way, it will be found that reversing the silk will help considerably in making the wings sit in the proper way.

Having tied in and cut off the waste stump of the hackle, continue winding the silk to the right until just a fraction of the bare shank of the hook remains exposed (Fig. 47).

The beginner will experience some difficulty in judging the proper amount of shank to be left over to the right of the hackle, and which will eventually form the head of the fly. The natural tendency at first will be to leave too little. Subsequently, it will be to leave too much ! As a matter of fact, it requires some nicety of judgment (being subject to varying proportions according to the type of fly being dressed), and even an expert always has to exercise care in leaving just the proper amount. Where the winging is heavy—*i.e.*, where a lot of material has to be tied in at this point—the proportion of shank left bare has to be greater relatively than where the winging is light, the two extremes being the Jock Scott on the one hand, and any sort of grub on the other. A small, neat head, as I have already remarked on more than one occasion, is a hallmark of high-class work ; but this must not, as not uncommonly happens, be secured at the expense of other essential qualities. It is quite easy to make a small, neat head, but not easy to combine this with firmness and durability. That is why it is so important that every turn of the silk must be made to tell ; there must be no superfluity ; therefore due importance must be attached to the use of none but fine, strong, and carefully-waxed silk—*fine*, because it " grips " so very much better than stout silk, *strong* for obvious reasons, and *carefully waxed*, because one turn of carefully waxed silk is of more use than ten turns of badly waxed silk.

I make no excuse for this digression, because the points therein touched upon are of some considerable practical importance.

To resume. Hitch the silk between the gut loop and the small portion of bare hook-

shank still left exposed, and wind in tight and
even coils in the *reverse* way back until the
roots of the hackle are reached.   These coils
of silk form what is known as the "bed" or
foundation for the wings, which it is necessary
to form for every kind of wing.

Now take two strips, exactly matching, and
carefully placed one on top of the other, and

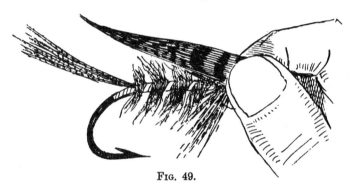

FIG. 49.

measure the required length, as shown in
Fig. 49.   (In strip-wings generally the wings
should not project much beyond the hook—
i.e., beyond a line drawn at right angles to the
shank, and just touching the bend, like the
tangent of a circle.   In Spey flies there should
be no part of the wing to the left of or posterior
to this line.)

Grip the strips, keeping them in a horizontal position with the left forefinger and thumb (Fig. 50), and then tie them in with precisely

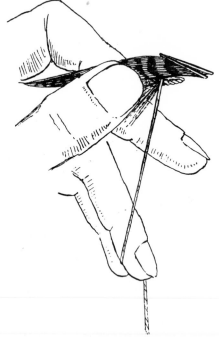

FIG. 50.

the same manipulation described in tying in the tail; not forgetting, of course, that the turns of silk in this case will be in the opposite direction—*i.e.*, over the hook and *towards* you.

The first turn of silk. should be close up to the hackle, and the next and subsequent turns closely, evenly, and firmly applied to the right.

As in tying in the tail (by the same coaxing manipulation with forefingers and thumbs), it is most important to keep the feathers all the time in a vertical position.

The set of the wings and the position of their waste ends should be as shown in Fig. 51, in which the left strip forms the right wing, and *vice versa*.

Three or four turns of silk to the right should be sufficient if tightly applied.

Cut off the waste ends of the wings both together on a slant with the curved-bladed scissors, and continue winding the silk to the right, until the extreme end of the shank is reached. Wind back to the left until the root of the wings is reached, and then again to the right until about three turns from the end, at which point apply the whip finish. Cut off the silk, smooth the head round, and apply varnish. The completed fly is shown on Plate XII., Fig. i. Fig. ii. on the same plate shows the same pattern tied in the same way, but with the *right* strip forming the right wing, and *vice versa*.

(ii.) In this method each wing is tied in separately,. and the turns of silk which tie in each wing are in exactly opposite directions to

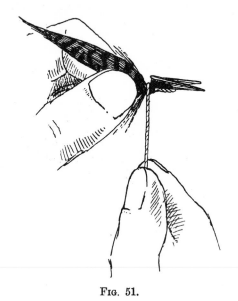

FIG. 51.

each other; that is to say, the silk is reversed for tying in the second wing.

Measure the proper length of the right wing by laying the "left" strip along the side of the hook nearest to you, as in Fig. 52. Hold the

strip in the position indicated lightly but firmly
with the right thumb, the left forefinger being
at the same time juxtaposed on the far side of
the hook, and having formed the foundation
for the wings as before, but in this case winding the silk in the same direction all the time
—*i.e.*, over the hook and *away* from you—tie
in the strip with one turn immediately in front
of the roots of the hackle. Hold the silk " in

FIG. 52.

catch," and examine (Fig. 53). The tendency
of the silk is to bring the upper edge of the
strip too far over. · If this is so (and it is safe
to assume that it *will* be so at first), the strip
must be coaxed, partly by pressing its upper
edge at the point where it is tied in towards
you with the right thumb-nail, and partly by
pulling in turn the portions of the strip on
each side of the silk towards you and down-

wards, until its upper edge exactly coincides
with an imaginary line bisecting the hook
longitudinally in two equal halves—*i.e.*, the
middle line (see pp. 16, 17, 18, and Fig. 2 on p. 17)
—so as to leave an equivalent portion of the silk
foundation to be occupied by the left wing.

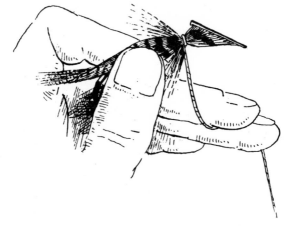

Fig. 53.

Having secured the proper set of the wing,
as just indicated, take two more turns of silk
to the right, being careful to see that the waste
end of the strip is not allowed to encroach
upon that portion of the foundation on the
far side of the imaginary line referred to by

giving it a downward pull after each turn of silk.

Now, holding the silk "in catch," lay on the left wing to correspond with the right, holding it in position with the left forefinger.

The next manipulation requires a little nicety and some practice to acquire proficiency in. It reverses the silk and secures the wing with the same movement. It is worth mastering, as it achieves simultaneously neatness, firmness, and a good " set."

Release the silk from " catch," taking in a loop round the tip of the middle finger of the left hand, and bring it round over the hook and towards you. Careful pressure downwards with the left middle finger, steadied by a controlling pull with the forefinger and thumb of the right hand holding the silk, will, with practice, secure the left wing in the correct position (Fig. 54). Swing the loop under the hook to the left by flexing the middle finger of the left hand, and take three or four close tight turns of silk to the left. This will, or should, bring it to the point where the first turn of silk secured the right wing. Release the left middle finger from the loop, and bring the latter to lie on the top of the shank and exactly coinciding with the line of junction of the upper edges of both wings, where, after being twisted and pulled tight, it may be cut off close.

The principles of this manipulation are diffi-

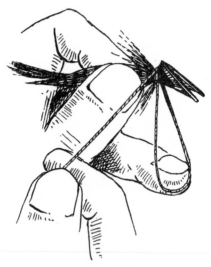

Fig. 54.

cult to describe in words, but can, perhaps, be understood by studying the diagrams (Figs. 55, 56, and 57), which illustrate it on a magnified scale.

All that remains to be done now is to cut

off the waste ends of the wings—each *separately* and on a slant, so that they meet at a

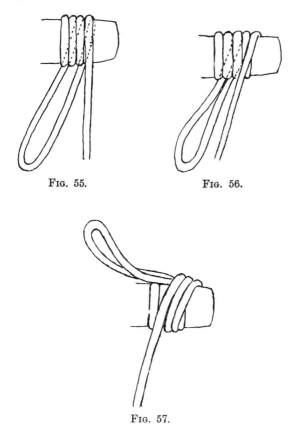

Fig. 55. Fig. 56.

Fig. 57.

point on the top of a shank—and tie them in with the silk, which may be finished off in

F

the usual way. (The complete fly is shown on Plate XII., Fig. iii.)

The same manipulations will apply, of course, when " right " strips are employed for right wings, and *vice versa*. (See Fig. iv., Plate XII.)

CHAPTER X

IN addition to a difference in the winging and in the body, this pattern presents fresh features to the fly-dresser in the matter of its tag and tail and in the possession of a butt.

As before, collect and prepare the materials required beforehand. These will be—

(1) Silver thread and lemon-coloured floss silk—about 2 inches of each for a $1\frac{1}{2}$-inch iron —for the tag.

(2) A small Golden Pheasant topping and an Indian Crow feather for the tail. Prepare the former by stripping off all the opaque fibres at the root, and (if necessary) manipulating it into the proper " set " by a series of nicks with the thumb-nail against the index-finger, holding it in the meanwhile by the base with the thumb

141

and forefinger of the other hand. This is impossible to explain in writing, and can only be understood by a practical demonstration. The beginner will save himself trouble if he chooses a topping that requires no " licking into shape," and will accordingly make his selection from the central part of the Golden Pheasant's crest (Fig. 58). Toppings with very pronounced curves are not, in my opinion, the

Fig. 58.　　　　Fig. 59.

most suitable for tails. The tail in the figures illustrating this lesson has about the correct curve, and is of the correct length. The fluffy fibres at the base of the Indian Crow feather, instead of being stripped, should be cut carefully and closely up to the central quill, as shown in Fig. 59. This method of preparation will apply to all feathers of a similar kind — *e.g.*, Blue Chatterer, Toucan,

Jungle Cock—whether used as tails, cheeks, or sides. It will be found that they will be much easier to tie in, and will " set " more satisfactorily when cut in this fashion than when stripped.

(3) A strand from a black Ostrich plume, commonly known as herl. This must be stripped clean for a short distance from the base, and will figure as the butt (Fig. 60).

(4) (*a*) Broad silver tinsel (about 2 inches), prepared in the same way as in the previous lesson (*q.v.*), for the ribs; and (*b*) fine silver twist as an additional rib to go behind (*a*), the object of

Fig. 60.

this twist being to protect the body hackle.

(5) Black floss silk (about 6 inches) for the body.

(6) A black cock's hackle doubled, as already described in the first lesson.

(7) A dark blue dyed cock's hackle for the throat, similarly prepared.

(8) Two feathers from a Jungle Cock's neck, carefully selected from opposite sides to match each other, and prepared in the same way as described in the case of the Indian Crow

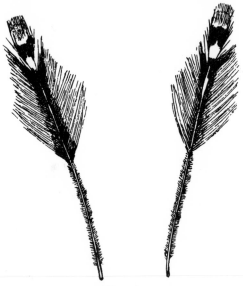

Fig. 61.

feather (Fig. 61).   These will be used for the inner wings.

(9 Two pairs of feathers from the Golden Pheasant's neck, commonly called tippets, one pair to be of larger size than the other.   Each size should be chosen from opposite sides, and

the bases of all should be stripped clean and nicked on the stem at the point where they will be tied in. The point of tying in, of course, is determined by measurement on the hook (see Fig. 73, which shows the correct

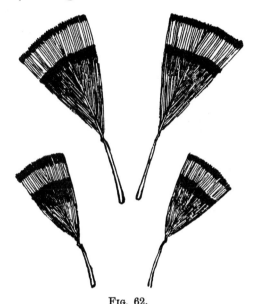

Fig. 62.

length for the wing). The smaller tippets should correspond in size exactly with that portion of the larger tippets, which is limited by the first bar of the fibres (see Fig. 62). These four tippets form the outer or covering wings.

(10) Two small Jungle Cock's feathers and two feathers from a Blue Chatterer for the cheeks (Fig. 63), each prepared in the way already described.

(11) A topping to go over the wings (Fig. 64). This should be stripped similarly to the one selected for the tail, and, in addition, must be nicked at the point where it is going to be tied in. It is an advantage in addition

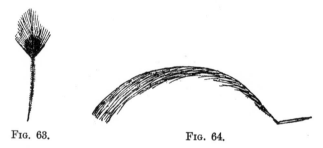

FIG. 63.　　　　FIG. 64.

to flatten the stem laterally beyond the nick by drawing it between the thumb-nail and forefinger firmly pressed together.

(12) Two fibres from opposite sides of the centre tail feather of a Blue and Yellow Macaw for the horns.

In this pattern a foundation is required for the tag. Accordingly the dressing silk is carried down the bend of the hook until a

point immediately over the barb is reached.
Here tie in the silver thread in such a way
that the portion to the right will be along the
under surface of the shank (Fig. 65). Wind
the silk back to the right for about six turns
tightly, evenly, and very closely (it is most
important in this variety of tag that the turns
of silk should be very close and very even).

FIG. 65.

Then wind the thread over the coils of silk
(one turn over the bare shank first), also in
close and even turns, pressing each turn upon
the preceding one with the thumb-nail, so as
to make sure that nothing but the thread will
be visible. When four or five turns of thread
have been taken, secure it with the dressing
silk, and cut off in the same way as described
in the first lesson for the oval ribbing tinsel,

the waste end of the thread lying along the under surface of the shank.

Wind the dressing silk closely and evenly to the right until the part to be occupied by the butt is reached, when the lemon floss must be tied in. One turn of the dressing silk ought to be sufficient to secure the floss, the free end of which should be tapered, and

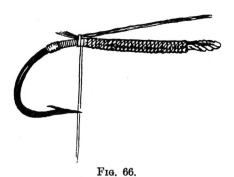

Fɪɢ. 66.

should lie on the upper surface of the hook, as shown in Fig. 66. Hitch the dressing silk (see Fig. 34), and then completely cover the foundation of dressing silk to the right of the thread with carefully applied turns of the floss to the left, and then back to the right. Unhitch the dressing silk, and fix the floss (subsequently pulling it tight) with two or

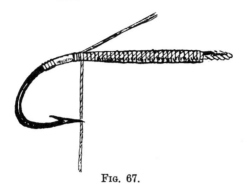

FIG. 67.

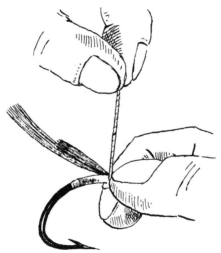

FIG. 68.

three turns of the dressing silk to the right (Fig. 67). Cut off the waste end of the floss close.

Wind the dressing silk back for three turns
to the left, and tie in the small topping
(Fig. 58) with one turn of silk, keeping it on
the top of the hook-shank in the correct posi-

FIG. 69.

tion with the right thumb-nail. With the
subsequent turn of silk tie in the Indian Crow
feather (Fig. 59) in the same way, taking care
that it lies quite flat, with the "best" surface
uppermost (Fig. 68). With one tight turn of

silk tie in the Ostrich herl, the portion of the
quill to which the " fluff" is attached being to
the left—*i.e.*, pointing towards the tail (see
Fig. 69). Wind two or three more turns of
silk towards the right, and having hitched it,
proceed to form the butt by taking first one

FIG. 70.

turn of herl to the left up to where the floss
silk ends, and then covering this with close
even turns towards the right. Unhitch the
dressing silk, and with one turn tie in the
herl, pulling the latter tight at the same time
(Fig. 70).

Now tie in the silver tinsel and twist for
the ribbing simultaneously, keeping the twist
on the under surface of the hook-shank. Continue tying towards the right with the dressing
silk in close even coils, covering up in turn the
waste ends of the tinsel, twist, herl, and tail
respectively, cutting these off carefully, on a
slant where necessary, so as to insure a proper
taper for the body, until the point where the
throat will be tied in is reached. Here tie in
the back floss silk for the body with one turn
of dressing silk, laying the free end of the floss,
properly cut on a slant beforehand to continue
the necessary taper, underneath the shank of
the hook (Fig. 71). Hitch the silk and wind
the floss to the left in wide, even turns. Some
little distance before the butt is reached tie
in the body hackle with the floss silk (Fig. 72),
and then continue winding down to the butt
(but not including the hackle), and back again
towards the head, completely covering both
the dressing silk and the previous coils of floss.
A floss silk body should be quite smooth, free
from all bumps or irregularities, and should
taper very gradually from butt to head. It
will greatly help in securing this effect if the

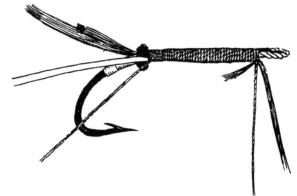

FIG. 71.

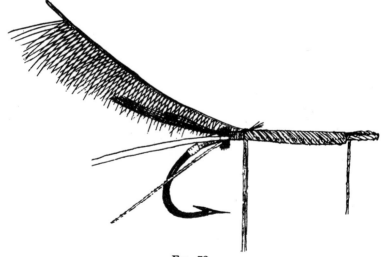

FIG. 72.

floss silk with each turn is kept out of the twist, and wound on in broad, ribbon-like coils. But this is a question of manipulation, which can only be acquired by practice, and is not learnt from written directions. A body of floss silk is tied in and finished off in the same way as is the ribbing of oval tinsel described in the second lesson.

The flat silver tinsel ribbing is then wound round, and immediately behind this the twist, the usual number of turns being in each case five. Both are finished off with turns of silk towards the head, and the waste ends cut off in the usual way (the twist being analogous to oval tinsel in this respect). The dressing silk is then wound back to the left over the previous coils, which finished off the tinsel and twist, a foundation being thus formed for the throat. (It is most important that each turn of both ribbings should be pulled tight.)

The hackles are now wound round and finished off in the usual way, each turn of the ribbing hackle, of course, fitting close up to each turn of the twist. The first turn of the ribbing hackle is usually just behind the second turn of the ribbing tinsel.

Before tying in the wings, it is a good plan to press down on either side of the hook the upstanding fibres of the hackles, so as to leave a clear space along the upper surface of the hook-shank. This will facilitate the comfortable set of the wings, particularly in the case of whole-feather wings.

Form the foundation for the wings as described in the previous lesson, and, *with the silk reversed*, tie in the larger pair of Jungle Cock feathers, which must first have been accurately placed together back to back, carefully measured and nicked in the stems at the point to be tied in. As in the case of all whole-feather wings, these should be fixed both at the same time with the same turns of silk, and they should lie on edge and absolutely on the top of the hook (Fig. 73). The position of the hands during the process will be the same as described and figured in the tying in of the tail and of the upright wings of the pattern in the previous lesson (see Fig. 45). With a little practice, two turns of silk, if well waxed, should be sufficient.

Now lay on the larger pair of tippets, also

nicked at the point of tying in, one on each side of the Jungle Cock feathers. The tippets are placed separately, but tied in together. Three turns of silk should be sufficient.

Lay on the smaller pair of tippets, and then

Fig. 73.

the smaller pair of Jungle Cock feathers, and in turn tie these in in the same way. The stem of each feather at the point where it is tied in should be at the side of, and not on the top of, the feather immediately preceding it, and each turn of silk should be to the right.

By the time both pairs of tippets and both
pairs of Jungle Cock feathers have been tied
in there should still be a small piece of hook-
shank uncovered to the right of the silk, and
all the waste stumps should be lying on the
top of the shank, as indicated in Fig. 74, which
also shows the silk wound back to the left and

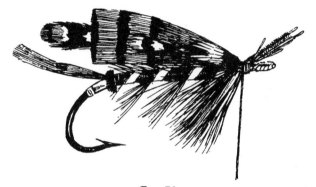

the Blue Chatterer cheeks tied in, these latter,
like the other paired feathers, being placed
immediately to the side of, but covering the
bases of, the preceding small Jungle Cock
feathers.

Cut off the stumps close up to the bare
piece of shank slightly on a slant with the
curved-bladed scissors, at the same time press-

ing the gut loop down (in the manner shown in Fig. 87).

Now tie in the topping (Fig. 64). It will help in the correct set of the topping if, in addition to being flattened, the stem, a short distance beyond the nick, is cut on either side to a point. To get the topping to sit nicely will be rather troublesome at first. In this, as in everything else, practice is necessary, though the desired result will be achieved much more readily if care has been taken in tying the wings to keep the structure on which the topping rests as smooth and as even as possible.

Tie in the topping with continuous and even turns of silk towards the extreme tip of the shank, and entirely cover the latter now, having previously cut off any waste stump of topping projecting beyond. Wind back to the left over the entire length of the head, and then tie in the horns of Blue and Yellow Macaw immediately to the right of, and somewhat above, the Blue Chatterer cheeks. The set of the horns should be inclined to the vertical. Three turns of silk towards the right should suffice to give a firm attachment to the horns. Cut off the waste ends of the latter close, and then continue winding the silk towards the right. Finally, finish off with the whip finish as usual, and varnish the head. The pattern is now completed (see Plate V.).

CHAPTER XI

THE FIFTH LESSON—A MIXED-WINGED PATTERN,
WITH A PLAIN FLAT TINSEL BODY (*e.g.*,
SILVER DOCTOR)

THE additional features in this pattern are—
(*a*) the woollen butt; (*b*) the woollen head;
(*c*) the flat tinsel body; and (*d*) the mixed
wing.

The materials required up to the winging
stage will be—

(1) Silver thread and lemon floss for the tag.
(2) A topping and Blue Chatterer feather
    for the tail.
(3) Scarlet Berlin wool for the butt.
(4) Flat silver tinsel for the body.
(5) Oval silver tinsel for the ribs.
(6) A pale blue dyed cock's hackle for
    the first throat.
(7) A barred Widgeon feather for the
    second throat.

In this and in subsequent lessons I propose to deal only with the details of manipulation not hitherto considered, as otherwise it would merely be a repetition of what has gone before ; and, besides, I am assuming that the reader will by now be more or less familiar with the main principles governing the position of the hands and the handling of the hook, silk, and materials generally.

The butt is formed thus : Unravel a piece of scarlet Berlin wool, and select a strand

FIG. 75.

therefrom about 2 inches in length Break this up in the fingers into small pieces, and, having thoroughly disintegrated it, shape it into the form of a spindle, and spin it on to the dressing silk (Fig. 75). When wound round the hook, the butt, when viewed from the side, should have the shape of an ellipse (see Figs. 76, 85, and 86).

The formation of the body will be difficult for the beginner. The gut loop will have to be tied in with particular care, and I would suggest that the reader might refer back to my remarks in Chapter VII.

Tie in the tinsels (flat and oval) as you would the tinsel and twist respectively for the Black Ranger in the preceding lesson, and see that the first turn of the silk over them lies

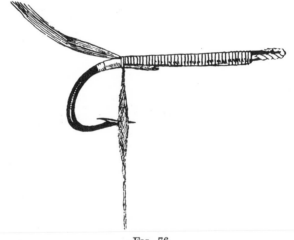

Fig. 76.

quite close up to the butt. The way in which the waste end of the oval ribbing tinsel is made to lie under the hook, and the care with which it is cut off and shaped, will determine to a very large extent whether the tinsel body will be a smooth success or otherwise. When winding towards the head, pull each turn of both tinsels tight with the right thumb and forefinger before taking the next turn, and give an extra tight pull before tying off with the dressing silk. Each turn of the flat tinsel must fit close up to the preceding turn, but *not under any circumstances must there be any overlapping.* Overlapping is fatal, not only to the appearance, but also to the durability of a flat tinsel body. A healthy kelt, with its serviceable dentition, will abundantly demonstrate the practical objection to overlapping tinsel or any other irregularity in a flat tinsel body.

Tie off the flat tinsel with about five turns of silk towards the left—*i.e.,* towards the tail of the fly—then tie off the oval tinsel with five turns of silk to the right over the preceding turns. Finish off as already described in a previous lesson. Figs. 77 and 78 illustrate these manipulations diagrammatically on a magnified scale. The turns of silk will subsequently go right up to, but not over, the bare hook-shank, and will then be wound back to the left until the tinsel body is reached once more. These turns of silk are a foundation for the throat hackles, which can now be put on in the usual way. Finish off and form the foundation for the head as usual. The pattern is now ready for the somewhat intricate process of winging.

Select the following feathers in " pairs " (or " centres," if available)—viz., tippet, Golden Pheasant tail, Bustard, Florican, Swan—natural white and dyed pale blue, scarlet, and lemon—

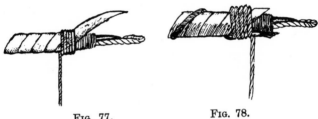

FIG. 77.   FIG. 78.

grey and cinnamon Turkey tail, Pintail, barred Summer Duck, brown Mallard, Macaw tail (blue and yellow), and a topping.

Twitch off opposite strips from the tippets (Fig. 79), and cut off opposite strips from the Golden Pheasant tail (Fig. 80).

Cut off single strands of each of the Bustard, Florican, Swan, and Turkey tail feathers, and lay each "left" strand side by side between the forefinger and thumb of the left hand, the tip of each strand projecting a little beyond the one immediately preceding it. Having collected in this manner as many strands as

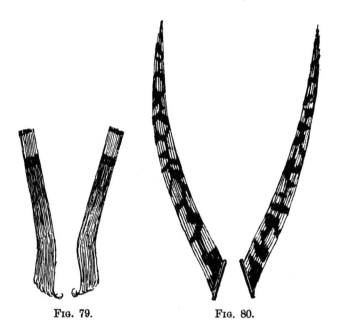

Fig. 79. Fig. 80.

the fingers can hold comfortably, grasp the bases together with the right forefinger and thumb, and, with a firm but gentle stroking movement of the retaining forefinger and thumb of the left hand upwards and to the left, make the strands adhere to each other

(see Fig. 81). This is a process known as
"marrying." Do likewise with another batch
of fibres, and "marry" these on to the first
batch. Then do the same with the "right"
strands. These "married" fibres constitute
a mixed-wing, "left" fibres usually forming

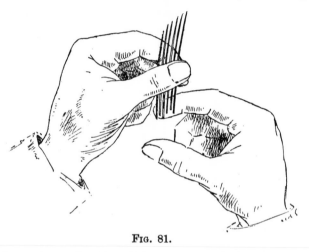

Fɪɢ. 81.

the right wing, and *vice versa*. The right and
left "sheaths" ready for laying on are shown
in Fig. 82. It is essential to the proper set of
the wings to curve or "hump" the "sheaths"
in the manner illustrated.

Now cut out "left" and "right" strips from
the Pintail, Summer Duck, and brown Mallard

feathers, and " marry " the corresponding strips
of the two former together, " left " strips for
the right wing, and *vice versa*, the Pintail
being placed so as to lie below the Summer
Duck (Fig. 83).

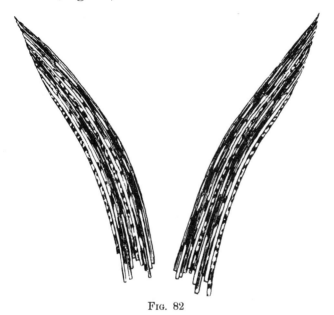

FIG. 82

The Mallard strips are put on last in the
formation of the wing, and in order to help
the curved shape of the wings the " left " strips
in this case are tied in on the *left* side and
vice versa (Fig. 84).

The subsequent manipulations are similar in general principle to those already described for the corresponding stages of previous patterns, and need not be further detailed. Lay on the tippet strips first, then the Golden Pheasant strips—" left " strips for right wings, and *vice versa* (Fig. 85), then the " sheaths," then the

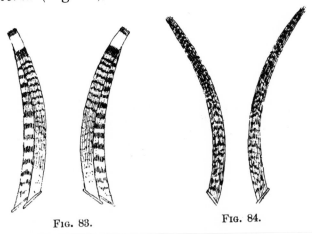

FIG. 83.   FIG. 84.

" married " Pintail and Summer Duck (to occupy about the middle of each wing), and finally the brown Mallard to lie on the upper edge, and to extend for the entire length of the wings.

The fly, after the topping and horns have been tied in, should have the appearance shown

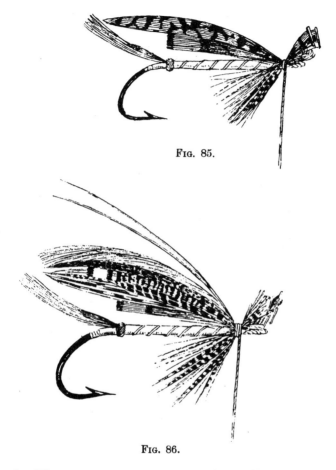

Fig. 85.

Fig. 86.

in Fig. 86. The Mallard strips will be found
to be rather obstreperous. They will tend to
set better if, before they are tied in, their bases

are insinuated in between the waste ends of the other various feathers and made to lie back to back among them.

Cut off the waste ends carefully on a slant (Fig. 87) and form the head. Do not, how-

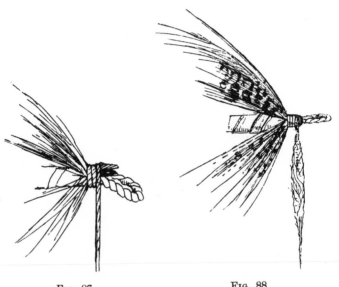

Fig. 87.   Fig. 88.

ever, in this case be at pains to secure a tapering head. Make it rather the shape of a very blunt-pointed rifle - bullet by taking more than the usual number of turns of silk immediately to the left of the gut loop. Without

finishing off, varnish the head and set it aside
for a while to dry. Prepare a piece of scarlet
Berlin wool as for the butt. Before the varnish
has become quite hard—*i.e.*, while still retaining some of its stickiness – spin the wool on
the silk (the latter being close up to the gut

FIG. 89.

loop, as shown in Fig. 88), and take three or
four turns to the left. The size of the wool-
spindle will have to be correctly judged so that
there shall be no more and no less than will
exactly reach to the roots of the wings. Finish
off the dressing silk at the roots of the wings
with the whip finish (the turns, however, in

this case being one on top of the other instead of side by side, so as to occupy as little space as possible) or with a succession of half hitches, and cut off close. Like the butt, the head should have the shape of an ellipse (Fig. 89). (For the completed fly, see Plate IV.)

CHAPTER XII

MATERIALS required :

(1) Silver tinsel, oval or flat (I prefer the latter), for the tag.

(2) A topping and Indian Crow feather for the tail.

(3) Black Ostrich herl for the butts.

(4) Twelve of the golden yellow feathers from the breast of a Toucan for veiling the posterior joint of the body.

(5) Lemon floss for the posterior joint, and black floss for the anterior joint.

(6) Oval silver tinsel ribbing for the posterior joint, flat silver and silver twist for the ribs of the anterior joint.

173

(7) A natural black or dyed black cock's hackle for ribbing the anterior joint.

(8) A speckled Gallina feather for the throat.

(9) " Right " and " left " strips from a black white-tipped Turkey's tail feather for the under-wings.

(10) " Right " and "left" strands of scarlet, lemon, and blue dyed Swan, Bustard, Florican, cinnamon and grey Turkey tail, and green Peacock sword feather, and " right " and " left " strips of Teal, barred Summer Duck, and brown Mallard—for the built wings.

(11) Two Jungle Cock feathers for the sides.

(12) Two Blue Chatterer feathers for the cheeks.

(13) A topping.

(14) Two Blue and Yellow Macaw tail strands for the horns to go over all.

This is one of the most difficult patterns to dress, and to dress it well constitutes a test of ability.

There will be no object in describing the

dressing in detail, however, and I will merely mention one or two points which appear to me important, and specific mention of which has not already been made.

A plain tag of oval tinsel is tied in precisely the same way as the thread of a mixed tag described in the fourth lesson, but, of course, the tinsel is carried right up to where the butt begins.

The Toucan feathers (six of which are used above and six below the posterior joint of the body) are prepared in the same manner as Indian Crow, Blue Chatterer, etc.; but as these feathers possess a natural curve, which is rather pronounced, it is rather important to choose them of a size proportionate to the size of the fly to be dressed, otherwise they will not lie nicely, and will be difficult to tie in properly. Tie in each set together, placing the six feathers exactly one on top of each other, and moistening them previously to keep them together. Press down the stems at the point of tying in against the hook-shank with the right thumb-nail, and, before winding the silk round, see that the stems are not displaced from one another.

In tying the under pair of wings it will be
an advantage to use " left " strips for the left
wing, and *vice versa*. The " set " thus produced, being rather horizontal, will help you
to keep a portion of the white tip showing
beneath the superimposed built wings, which
is, of course, what is desired, and which, in
fact, is a feature without which the Jock Scott

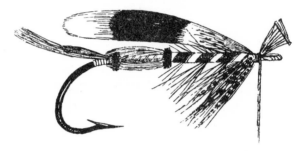

Fig. 90.

loses half the attraction of its appearance (see
Fig. 90).

Tie in the " married " fibres of—(*a*) dyed
Swan, (*b*) Bustard and Florican, (*c*) cinnamon
and grey Turkey tail, and (*d*) the strands of Peacock sword feather, in that order, from below
upwards, taking care that the white-tipped
inner pair of wings is never allowed to be
obscured, and that the succeeding instalments

of " married " strands do not entirely hide those
which have preceded them.   This will not be
easy even to an expert.   " Humping " the
strands before laying on, gripping them firmly
with the left forefinger and thumb when laid on,
and lifting the stumps upwards, so as to lie
back to back above the end of the hook-shank
before tying in, will help considerably in securing the proper set of the second and third
batches of " married " strands.   Each batch
must be tied in with turns of the silk immediately in front of the hackle ; that is to say, the
silk will need to be coiled back to the left after
each batch has been tied in.   A rather lumpy
head is the inevitable consequence in the smaller
sizes of this pattern.

A manœuvre which further helps to keep
the component parts of the wings " humped "
is to pull the turn of silk which ties them in
downwards *and to the left* rather than straight
downwards.

The " married " strips of Teal and Summer
Duck are then tied in, so as to occupy the
central portion of each wing, and to extend
backwards as far as the butt.

The Mallard strips (" right " for the right

wing, and *vice versa*) are tied in as described in
the preceding lesson.

The Jungle Cock sides and the Blue Chatterer cheeks are then attached.   The topping
and   horns   are   tied   in   and   the   head   then
finished off in the usual way.

The reader will have to try to turn out a

FIG. 91.

Jock Scott as illustrated in Fig. 91, which is
a model of what a well-dressed Jock Scott
should be.   If he succeeds in doing so, he may
pat himself complacently on the back, for the
proportions and general symmetry are about
as near perfection as can be.   (The figure has
been drawn from an actual fly in my possession,
but I did not dress the fly myself.)

CHAPTER XIII

THE SEVENTH LESSON—A SPEY FLY (*e.g.*, GREEN KING)

THE peculiarities of this type of pattern have already been touched upon in Chapter II.

It will be logical as well as useful if the reader includes the dressing of this class of fly as a separate lesson. The manipulations in themselves do not present any peculiarity which has not already been dealt with, but the pattern is so out of the ordinary in appearance, and has a character so peculiar to itself, that it is well to treat it as distinct from other patterns.

The first point of importance to bear in mind is that the body should be as thin as possible. The type of hook usually employed is the light-ironed, long-shanked hook, which is a feature of the Dee strip-winged patterns. This type of hook is fine in the wire and, com-

paratively speaking, light. Accordingly, the
twisted gut for the loop may safely be less
stout than one would use in the ordinary
way, all of which, of course, is of help in the
construction of a thin body.

The next thing to be careful about is the
order in which the various materials are tied
in at the posterior end of the body.

The first to be tied in is the single strand of
the green Berlin wool for the body—with one
turn of silk towards the head. Another turn
of silk in the same direction secures the silver
twist for the protecting ribbing, and a third
turn the hackle (by the base and with one side
stripped). The " best " surface of the hackle
when this is about to be wound on should
face to the right—*i.e.*, towards the head of the
fly—and the side left unstripped will determine
the direction in which the hackle is to be
wound. The stem of the hackle should lie
either exactly on the top of the hook-shank
(as in Fig. 92), or exactly underneath it.

The waste ends of the wool and twist should
lie along and exactly underneath the shank.

Now tie in the flat silver tinsel at the side of
the hook-shank in the usual way, and subse-

quently, after eight or nine turns of silk, tie
in the flat gold tinsel in the same way (see
Fig. 92). Continue winding the silk up to
the right, and then hitch it. Only a small
portion of bare shank need be left exposed in

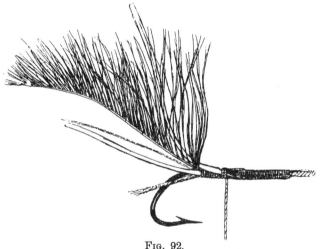

Fig. 92.

this type of fly, as the head must be kept
small, and the wings are merely single strips.

Wind the wool round the hook carefully,
closely, and as tightly as it will bear, up to the
head, and finish off; then the flat silver tinsel,
and after that the gold tinsel, the finishing off
turns of silk being *in each case continuously to*

the left, after which the silk must be wound back towards the head.

Now wind the hackle round so that the number of turns exceeds by one the number of turns of the tinsel. If wound in the same direction as the tinsel, each turn should occupy

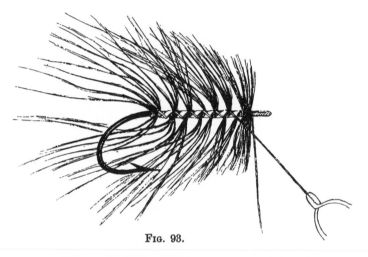

FIG. 93.

a position exactly midway between the turns of tinsel. At the point where the silk has finished off the tinsels take closer turns of the hackle and finish it off in the usual manner.

Wind the twist over the turns of the hackle *in the opposite direction in every case—i.e.,* if the hackle is going round over the hook-shank and *towards* you, the twist will be going over the hook-shank and *away* from you, and *vice versa*, as in Fig. 93. In winding the twist care must be taken not to tie in any of the fibres of the hackle. These should be separated carefully with a stiletto before each turn

Fig. 94.

of the twist is pulled tight. Only the central stem of the hackle is tied in.

A Widgeon or Teal feather ("doubled" in the customary manner) is used for the throat.

Finally, the Mallard wing strips ("right" strip for right wing, and *vice versa*) are tied in in precisely the same way as described on pp. 134 to 140. Be very particular to choose Mallard strips of the same length, and, if possible, from the corresponding portions of similarly coloured and similarly marked feathers of opposite sides. Spey fly wings should lie over the hook at a very horizontal inclination, and the relation of each wing to its fellow should be such that the effect produced is that of a keelless racing-boat placed upside down.

Connoisseurs of Spey flies attach great importance to the presence of the light grey roots to the wings, as shown in Fig. 94, and in most of the Spey flies in Plate VII.

The wings should not extend beyond the bend of the hook, and the head should be as small as possible.

CHAPTER XIV

THE characteristic features of this group of patterns are a general slimness and economy of dressing, and the peculiar set of the wings.

Even though the bodies of most of these flies are composed of Seal's fur, there is never the suggestion of bulk—at all events there should not be—so that when held up to the light the body proper shows as a thin core, so to speak, running through a kind of nebulous atmosphere formed by the freely picked out fur. This effect is attained by spinning the fur on rather loosely and pulling the turns of ribbing tinsel, which should be flat and comparatively broad, as tight as can be.

The wings are composed of simple strips from the tail feathers of certain breeds of domestic Turkey cocks, " right " strips always being employed for the right wing, and "left" strips for the left (Fig. 95).

Owing to the peculiar construction of the fibre of these feathers, the strips have to be put on in a manner somewhat different to that which applies, and which has already

Fig. 95.

been described, in the case of ordinary sloping or horizontal strip-wings (see pp. 134 to 140), as otherwise they would split. The object is to maintain as far as possible the coherence of the fibres of the strip as a whole, and this is possible only when the fibres are secured so

as to lie all practically in the same plane; that
is to say, at the point of tying in they are
squeezed together laterally by the silk, and
made to lie on the upper part of the hook
within a space representing an arc of a circle
considerably less than a semicircle (see p. 18
and Fig. 2).   This can be effected auto-

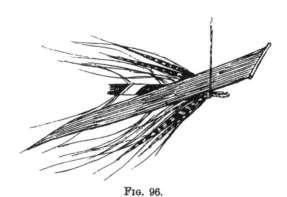

Fig. 96.

matically, after a little practice, in the following
manner :

Lay the " right " strip on as shown in Fig. 96,
having first taken a few turns with the dressing silk to the right *over the hook and away
from you* to form the foundation for the wings.
In doing so, measure the strip carefully, so
that only a small portion of what will even-

tually be the tip of the right wing project:
beyond the hook-shank. Holding the strip
firmly pressed against the hook with the left
thumb, take a turn of the silk over it, and to
the *left*. Hold the silk "in catch." The strip

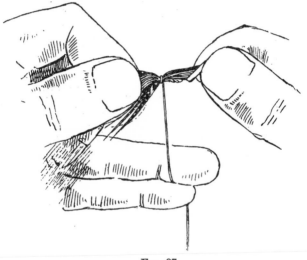

Fig. 97.

at the point where it is tied in by the silk will
now entirely occupy the top of the shank, and
will perhaps overlap to some extent on the far
side. The edge of the strip nearest to you
will be, or should be, correctly placed, but
it will be necessary to bring the edge farthest

away from you back, so that it will not encroach upon any part of the shank beyond the
" middle line " (see pp 16 and 17). This is done
by pulling towards you the distal portion of
the piece of quill cut off with the strip, all the
time holding the strip firmly against the shank
with the left thumb, and keeping the dressing

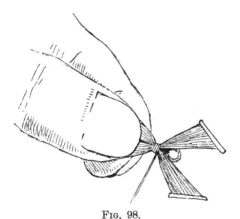

FIG. 98.

silk " in catch " (Fig. 97). Having thus adjusted the strip, take another turn of silk
towards the left, remove the left thumb, and
examine results. The strip should lie almost
flat along the body of the fly. Now reverse
the silk (see pp. 137, 138 and 139, and Figs. 55,
56, and 57), still going to the left, until the root

of the hackle is reached—*i.e.*, the point at which the " left " strip is to be tied in. Lay the " left " strip flat across the top of the hook-shank, having measured it first to correspond with its fellow of the opposite side, and keeping it in that position with the left thumb ; pressing down upon the hook (the left fore-finger being underneath on the other side of

F*ig*. 99.

the hook-shank), take a turn over it and to the right (with the silk going over and towards you this time, of course). Hold the silk " in catch," and adjust the strip by pulling on the attached piece of quill as before (but in the opposite direction). Take another turn of silk to the right (*i.e.*, towards the gut loop), disengage the retaining finger and thumb, and examine results. If the set of the strip is satisfactory, take a few more turns of silk towards the right, holding both strips flat on top of the hook and keeping the waste ends separated as shown in Fig. 98. Cut off the

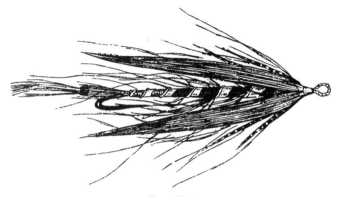

Fig. 100.

waste ends carefully, as in Fig. 99, and finish off as usual.

The finished article should be as in Fig. 100, which is a representation of a Dee strip-wing looked at from above.

CHAPTER XV

Herl-Wings.—These are either from the
sword feathers or from the moon feathers
of the Peacock.

The former are prepared by cutting off
corresponding strips from feathers of opposite
sides, with a portion of the central quill adhering, in just the same way as ordinary strip-
wings are prepared, and they are tied on both
together on the top of the hook-shank like any
upright wing. The " right " and " left " strips
may be employed respectively either for the
right and left wings, or *vice versa* (see Green
Peacock in Plate IX.).

Moon feather herl-wings may be prepared
like ordinary strip-wings, but more usually,
and especially in large flies, the strands of herl

are cut off from the central quill, and put on in a bunch, an equal number of strands for each side, on the top of the hook-shank— "like a bottle brush," as an expert fly-dressing friend of mine puts it (see Beauly Snow Fly in Plate VII.).

Topping-Wings.—These at first will be very difficult to put on satisfactorily, and even in the hands of an expert present difficulties.

They require careful preparation beforehand.

Fɪɢ. 101.

The toppings must be selected in such a way that there is a gradual lengthening from the undermost to the uppermost topping, and the stems, duly nicked at the point of tying in, must lie on the top of the hook-shank exactly in the "middle line," one immediately on top of the other. Fig. 101 shows the kind of shape the toppings when selected and prepared should assume before being tied on. They will be easier to keep in position if they are

moistened previously, and at first it will be
advisable not to attempt to tie them on all at
once with the same turn of silk (as an expert
would do), but to put them on in batches of
two or three at a time (see Variegated Sun
Fly in Plate IX. and Black Prince and Canary
in Plate V.).

Upright Mallard Wings. — Plain Mallard
wings are usually tied on horizontally, as explained in the winging of the March Brown on
pp. 128 and 130, style (II.) (*a*), and described
on pp. 134 to 140. But sometimes it is desired
to dress them upright, as in style (I.), (*a*) and
(*b*), of winging the March Brown (see pp. 129
to 134), and as it is exceedingly difficult to
dress these without displacing the fibres and
disturbing the continuity of the strips, it is a
good plan to tie in first two upright strips of
ordinary brown Turkey tail feathers, and then
to cover these with the strips of Mallard (see
Thunder and Lightning in Plate IX.).

Double Hackles.—These are just simply two
hackles (previously " doubled ") of different
colours, one placed within the other. In
winding them round the hook, care should be
taken that the stems of both are touching each

other all the time, otherwise the result will be unsightly (see Dreadnought in Plate I.).

Jay's Hackles. — By these are meant the vivid blue barred covert feathers from the wing of the common European Jay. They are extensively employed for throats, particularly in Irish patterns, and sometimes, though not so often, for body hackles. Only one side —the blue-barred side—is used, of course, the fibres on the other side being stripped. Mere stripping, however, will not be sufficient preparation, as the whole centre quill, which is stiff and coarse, will still remain. As much of this as possible will accordingly have to be removed. This is best and most easily done in the following manner: Lay the feather, best side undermost, along the edge of one of the sides of an open wooden box, and keep it there tightly stretched, with the forefinger of the left hand pressing upon the tip of the feather, and the thumb of the same hand upon the root of the stem. With a very sharp knife pare off carefully, in one continuous stroke if possible, that part of the central quill which projects above the fibres lying on either side of it. With the nail of the right thumb scrape away the residue of the pith so exposed from within the central quill. In order to avoid breaking the fibres, this should be done from the root towards the tip of the feather—*i.e.*, in the same direction as that in which the fibres are inclined. Strip off the fibres of the useless side from the small piece of quill remaining. The feather is now ready to wind on as a hackle. Left wing coverts will be wound in the same way as any other kind of throat hackle, but right wing coverts, of course, will have to be wound in the opposite direction, and, accordingly, the dressing silk will in this case have to be reversed.

Transferring Wings.—Very often a pattern will be put out of action—*e.g.*, through the breaking of the hook, the cracking of the gut loop, the unravelling of the body tinsel or hackle, and so forth—and yet retain wings and wing adjuncts capable of further service. It is possible to transfer the wings of such a pattern *holus-bolus* on to another hook of the same size, and thus enable them to continue a useful existence over a freshly tied body and hackles similar (or dissimilar, for that matter) to those which coexisted with them originally. As this spells economy, and as the due observance of economy is one of the virtues, it will perhaps be a useful thing to describe how it may be effected.

Hold the damaged pattern upside down between the left forefinger and thumb at the root of the wings, and with the point of a sharp knife slit the varnished head underneath right down to the twisted gut of the gut loop. If the dressing silk forming the head has been properly waxed and varnished in the first instance, the whole head with the entire wings *in situ* can be removed, and transferred to the fresh hook prepared to receive them, in much the same way as a saddle is placed on a horse's back. Having taken two or three tight turns of the dressing silk up to the roots of the wings and immediately to the left of the remains of the old varnished head, the latter is now removed by carefully levering it off with the right thumb-nail, care being taken to remove every piece of the old dressing silk. The ends so exposed of the component parts of the wings are then adjusted to their proper position, and covered over with the dressing silk, which is subsequently finished off in the usual way.   Usually a pattern provided with wings put on in this manner possesses a head very much smaller than it would be possible to produce in the ordinary way.   The topping-wing of the Canary in Plate V. was transferred from another fly in this manner (note the smallness of the head).

APPENDIX

A FEW USEFUL PATTERNS*

Hackle, unless specified, means a cock's hackle, and refers to the body or ribbing hackle, which, unless otherwise stated, always begins at the second turn of the ribbing tinsel or ribs.

Herl, unless otherwise stated, means Ostrich herl.

Floss means floss silk.

Jay, as a throat or a hackle, refers, of course, to the blue-barred wing coverts.

Tinsel, where not specified, means either flat or oval tinsel—according to choice.

Tippet invariably refers to the Golden Pheasant ruff feather.

Topping invariably refers to Golden Pheasant crest feather.

Twist means silver twist.

* The dressings are given in the usual fly-dressing phraseology. The component parts of each pattern are mentioned, of course, in the order in which they are tied in—*e.g.*, for tails " a topping and Jungle Cock" means that the Jungle Cock feather is placed (best surface uppermost) over the topping; "first half" of body means the posterior half; "pale orange, deep orange, fiery brown, and pale blue Seal's fur" for a body, means in that order from the posterior extremity towards the head; the materials for wings first mentioned refer to the portions first tied in—and so forth.

199

(A) GENERAL OR STANDARD FLIES.

I. *Simple Strip-Wings :*

1. **Black Spean** * (hook, ¾ to 1⅛ inches).

     Tag : Silver thread and lemon floss.

     Tail : A topping.

     Body : Black Seal's fur (left smooth).

     Ribs : Oval gold tinsel.

     Throat : Speckled Gallina.

     Wings : Brown Mallard strips (set horizontally).

2. **Blue Charm** * (hook, ¾ to 1½ inches).

     Tag : Silver thread and golden yellow floss.

     Tail : A topping.

     Butt : Black herl.

     Body : Black floss.

     Ribs : Oval silver tinsel.

     Throat : A deep blue hackle.

     Wings : Mottled brown Turkey tail strips (set upright) and narrow strips of Teal along the upper edge ; a topping over.

3. **Blue and Yellow Wasp** (hook, 1 to 2 inches).

     Tag : Silver tinsel.

     Tail : A topping and strands of Golden Pheasant breast feather.

     Butt : Black herl.

     Body : In two equal halves—first half, lemon Seal's fur ; second half, pale blue Seal's fur.

     Ribs : Oval silver tinsel.

     Hackle : Pale blue hackle from end of lemon fur.

* See Plate IX.

I. *Simple Strip-Wings—continued :*

    3. **Blue and Yellow Wasp** (hook, 1 to 2 inches)—
        continued :

        Throat : Lemon hackle.

        Wings : Cinnamon Turkey tail strips (set
        upright).

    4. **Blue Limerick*** (hook, $\frac{3}{4}$ to $1\frac{1}{2}$ inches).

        Tag : Silver tinsel.

        Tail : A topping.

        Butt : Black herl.

        Body : Pale blue floss.

        Ribs : Oval silver tinsel, or finer oval silver
        and gold tinsel together.

        Hackle : Pale blue hackle.

        Throat : Light Woodcock breast feather, or
        Bittern hackle (when obtainable).

        Wings : Yellow Swan strips (set upright).

        Cheeks : Blue Chatterer ; a topping over.

        Horns : Blue and yellow Macaw.

    5. **Bumbee** (hook, $\frac{3}{4}$ to $1\frac{1}{8}$ inches).

        Tag : Silver tinsel.

        Tail : A tuft of scarlet Berlin wool.

        Body : Orange Berlin wool for first third
        remainder black Berlin wool.

        Ribs : Oval silver tinsel.

        Throat : A cochybondhu hackle.

        Wings : Brown Mallard strips (set horizon-
        tally).

    6. **Claret Alder*** (hook, $\frac{3}{4}$ to $1\frac{1}{8}$ inches).

        Tag : Silver thread and light orange floss.

        Tail : A tuft of claret wool.

        * See Plate IX.

I. *Simple Strip-Wings—continued :*

6. **Claret Alder** * (hook, ¾ to 1⅛ inches)—*continued :*
    Body : Peacock herl.
    Ribs : Fine oval gold tinsel.
    Hackle : A dark claret hackle.
    Wings : Brown Mallard strips (set horizontally).

7. **Dreadnought** † (hook, 1½ to 3 inches).
    Tag : Gold tinsel.
    Tail : A topping and Indian Crow.
    Butt : Scarlet Seal's fur.
    Body : Oval silver tinsel in three equal portions—the first portion butted with fiery brown Seal's fur, the second portion with deep blue Seal's fur.
    Throat : "Doubled" magenta and deep blue hackles.
    Wings : Cinnamon Turkey tail strips (set upright).
    Sides : Jungle Cock.
    Horns : Scarlet Macaw.

8. **Furnace Brown** ‡ (hook, ¾ to 1½ inches).
    Tag : Silver thread and golden yellow floss.
    Tail : A topping and strands of tippet.
    Body : First quarter, bright orange Seal's fur ; the remainder, fiery brown Seal's fur (picked out rough).
    Ribs : Oval gold tinsel.
    Hackle : A furnace hackle.
    Wings : Brown Mallard strips (set horizontally).

* See Plate IX.   † See Plate I.   ‡ See Plate IX.

Silver Grey
Rosy Dawn
Jock Scott

Orange Parson
Dreadnought
Durham Ranger

Butcher
Candlestick-maker
Popham

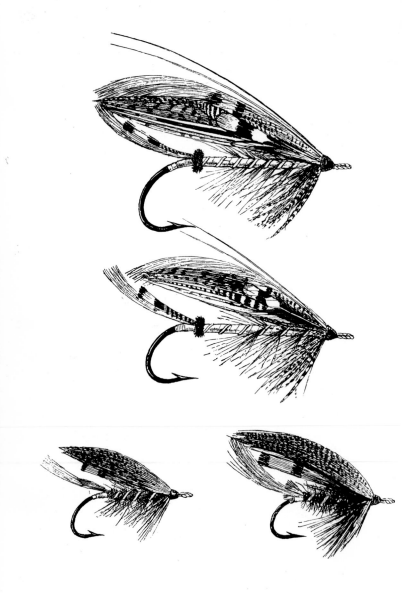

PLATE II. To illustrate "style".

Sir Richard 7/0

Benchill 6/0

Childers 5/0

PLATE III. GENERAL FLIES
(on large ordinary Limericks).

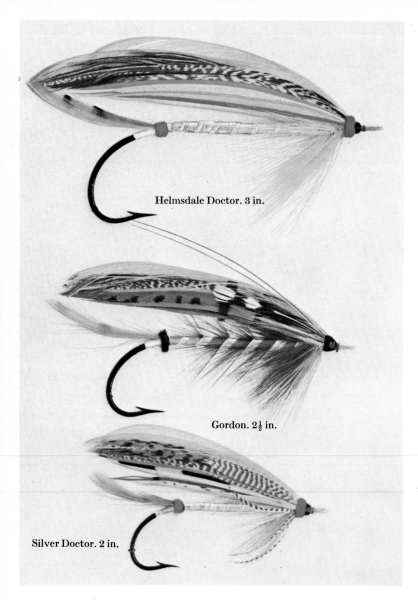

Helmsdale Doctor. 3 in.

Gordon. 2½ in.

Silver Doctor. 2 in.

PLATE IV. GENERAL FLIES
(on "Long Dees").

Group C

Black Ranger. 2 in.

Black Doctor. 1¾ in.

Dusty Miller. 1½ in.

Black Prince. 1¼ in.

Group B

Evening Star. 1¼ in.

Canary. 1½ in.

Torrish. 1¾ in.

Mar Lodge. 2 in.

PLATE V. GENERAL FLIES
(on "rational" irons).

Grey Eagle. 2½ in.

Glentana. 2 in.

Jock o' Dee. 2¼ in.

Akroyd (white winged). 2¾ in.

PLATE VII. SPEY FLIES, BEAULY SNOWFLY AND GRUBS

Carron. 1¾ in.
Grey Heron. 1¾ in.

Jungle Hornet. 1⅜ in.
Beauly Snowfly. 1¾ in.
Tippet Grub. 1½ in.

Green King. 1¾ in.
Purple King. 1¾ in

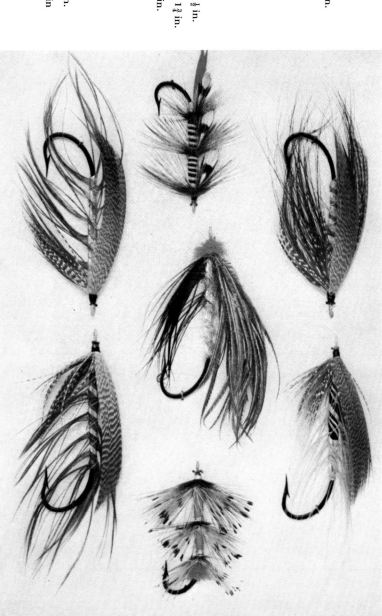

Half yellow and black
Black Goldfinch
Thunder and Lightning
(Irish).

Lemon and Grey
Half Grey and Brown
Lemon and Blue

Golden Olive
Claret Jay
Fiery Brown

PLATE VIII. IRISH PATTERNS
(on ordinary Limericks, no. 1).

Thunder and Lightning.
1⅛ in.

Silver Partridge. 1 in.

Jimmy. 1 in.

Furnace Brown. 1¼ in.

Grouse and Green 1⅛ in.

Silver, Blue and Jay. 1 in.

Variegated Sunfly. 1 in.

Claret Alder 1⅛ in.

Blue Limerick 1⅛ in.

Gold Sylph 1 in.

Green Peacock. 1 in.

Black Spean 1⅛ in.

Blue charm. 1⅛ in.

Glow-worm. 1 in.

Logie. 1 in.

March Brown. 1⅛ in.

PLATE IX. SMALL SUMMER PATTERNS

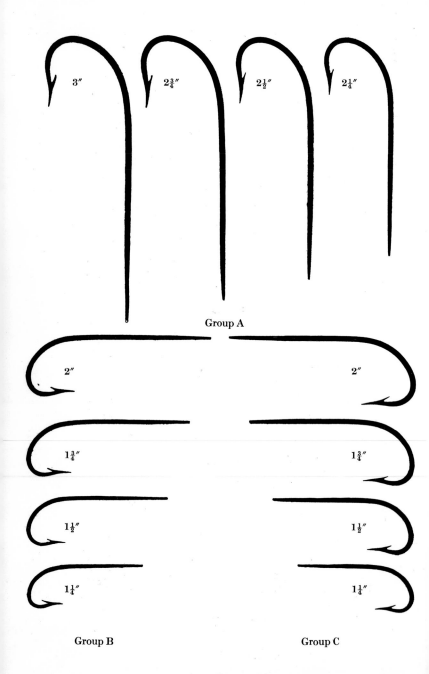

Group A

2″   2″

1¾″   1¾″

1½″   1½″

1¼″   1¼″

Group B   Group C

PLATE X.

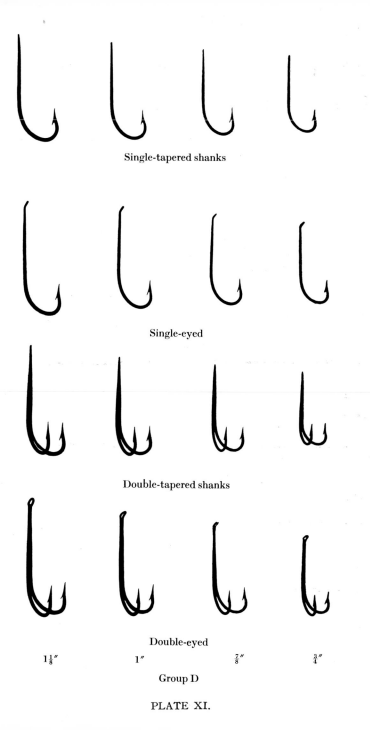

Single-tapered shanks

Single-eyed

Double-tapered shanks

Double-eyed

| $1\frac{1}{8}''$ | $1''$ | $\frac{7}{8}''$ | $\frac{3}{4}''$ |

Group D

PLATE XI.

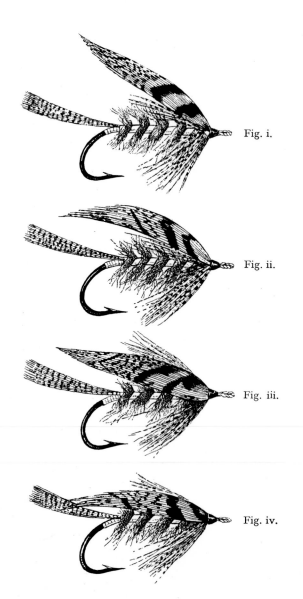

PLATE XII. FOUR DIFFERENT WAYS OF WINGING A MARCH BROWN

Adjutant

Black Joke

Blue Joke

PLATE XIII

Candlelight

Embers

Wrack

PLATE XIV

Bonny Charles

Springtime

Ballater

PLATE XV

Red Ranger

Green Hornet

Autumn Gold

PLATE XVI

I. Simple Strip-Wings—continued :

9. **Gold Sylph** * (hook, ¾ to 1⅛ inches).

> Tail : A topping and the tip of a Cock of the Rock feather.
>
> Body : Flat gold tinsel.
>
> Ribs : Fine oval silver tinsel.
>
> Throat : A lemon hackle followed by a Golden Pheasant's breast feather.
>
> Wings : Brown Mallard strips (set horizontally—Spey fashion).

10. **Jeannie** (hook, ¾ to 1⅛ inches).

> Tag : Silver tinsel.
>
> Tail : A topping.
>
> Body : First third lemon floss, remainder black floss.
>
> Ribs : Oval silver tinsel.
>
> Throat : A (natural) black hackle.
>
> Wings : Brown Mallard strips (set upright).
>
> Sides : Jungle Cock.

11. **Jimmie** * (hook, ¾ to 1⅛ inches).

> Tag : Silver tinsel.
>
> Tail : A topping.
>
> Body : In two equal halves — first half, bright orange floss ; second half, black floss.
>
> Ribs : Oval silver tinsel.
>
> Throat : A (natural) black hackle.
>
> Wings : Mottled brown Turkey tail strips (set upright).
>
> Cheeks : Jungle Cock.

* See Plate IX.

H

I. *Simple Strip-Wings—continued :*

12. **Jockie** (hook, ¾ to 1⅛ inches).

> Tag : Silver tinsel.
> Tail : A topping and Indian Crow.
> Body : First third, golden yellow floss ; remainder, dark claret floss.
> Ribs : Oval silver tinsel.
> Throat : A cochybondhu hackle.
> Wings : Brown Mallard strips (set upright).
> Sides : Jungle Cock.

13. **Joe Brady** (hook, ¾ to 1½ inches).

> Tag : Silver thread and lemon floss.
> Tail : A topping.
> Body : Flat silver tinsel.
> Ribs : Fine oval silver tinsel.
> Throat : A grass-green hackle.
> Wings : Cinnamon Turkey tail strips (set upright).
> Cheeks : Indian Crow ; a topping over.

14. **Logie*** (hook, ¾ to 1⅛ inches).

> Tag : Silver tinsel.
> Tail : A topping.
> Body : First two-fifths, pale primrose floss ; remainder, ruby red floss.
> Ribs : Fine oval silver tinsel.
> Throat : A pale blue hackle.
> Wings : Yellow Swan strips (set upright) slightly covered by brown Mallard strips.

15. **March Brown*** (hook, ¾ to 1½ inches).

> Tag : Silver tinsel.
> Tail : Unbarred Summer Duck.

* See Plate IX.

I. *Simple Strip-Wings—continued :*

15. **March Brown*** (hook, ¾ to 1½ inches)—*continued :*
    Body : Fur from a hare's face (well picked out).
    Ribs : Flat silver tinsel (comparatively broad).
    Throat : Partridge back (or rump in the larger sizes).
    Wings : Hen Pheasant tail strips (*usually* set horizontally).

16. **Silver, Blue and Jay*** (hook, ¾ to 1 inch).
    Tail : A topping.
    Body : Flat silver tinsel
    Throat : A pale blue hackle.
    Wings : Jay wing feather (secondaries) strips (set either horizontally or upright).

17. **Silver, Lemon and Jay** (hook, ¾ to 1 inch).
    Tail : A topping and Cock of the Rock in strands.
    Body : Flat silver tinsel.
    Throat : Lemon hackle.
    Wings : Golden Pheasant breast feather in strands covered by strips of Jay wing feather (secondaries) (set upright).

18. **Silver White** (hook, ¾ to 2 inches).
    Tag : Silver thread and lemon yellow floss.
    Tail : A topping and barred Summer Duck in strands.
    Butt : Black herl.
    Body : Flat silver tinsel.
    Ribs : Fine oval tinsel.
    Hackle : A badger hackle.

* See Plate IX.

I. *Simple Strip-Wings—continued :*

18. **Silver White** (hook, ¾ to 2 inches)—*continued :*
    Throat : Widgeon (or grey Partridge in the smaller sizes).
    Wings : White Swan strips (set upright).
    Cheeks : Jungle Cock.

19. **Teal and Red** (hook, ¾ to 1⅛ inches).
    Tag : Silver thread and lemon floss.
    Tail : A topping.
    Body : Two turns of bright orange Seal's fur ; remainder, bright scarlet Seal's fur.
    Hackle : A furnace or fiery brown hackle.
    Ribs : Oval silver tinsel.
    Wings : Teal, Widgeon, or Pintail strips (set horizontally).

20. **Thunder and Lightning*** (hook, 1 to 1¾ inches).
    Tag : Silver thread and golden yellow floss.
    Tail : A topping and Indian Crow.
    Butt : Black herl.
    Body : Black floss.
    Ribs : Oval gold tinsel.
    Hackle : A deep orange hackle.
    Throat : Jay.
    Wings : Brown Mallard strips (set upright).
    Cheeks : Jungle Cock ; a topping over.
    Horns : Blue and yellow Macaw.

21. **Toppy** (hook, 1 to 1½ inches).
    Tag : Silver tinsel.
    Tail : A topping and Indian Crow.
    Butt : Claret Seal's fur.

* See Plate IX.

I. *Simple Strip-Wings—continued :*

21. **Toppy** (hook, 1 to 1½ inches)—*continued :*

Body : First half, deep red floss butted with a crimson hackle; second half, black floss.

Ribs : Oval silver tinsel.

Throat : A black hackle.

Wings : Bronze white-tipped Turkey tail strips (set upright).

22. **White Wings** (hook, 1¼ to 2 inches).

Tag : Silver tinsel.

Tail : A topping and tippet in strands.

Body : Lemon yellow, bright orange, claret and black Seal's fur in equal sections (picked out).

Ribs : Broad silver tinsel and twist.

Hackle : A black or dark claret hackle.

Throat : A deep blue hackle.

Wings : White Swan strips (set horizontally).

II. *Whole-Feather Wings :*

1. **Avon Eagle** (hook, 2 to 3 inches).

Tag : Silver tinsel.

Tail : A topping and the tip of a Golden Pheasant's breast feather (best side under).

Body : Lemon, bright orange, scarlet and fiery brown Seal's fur in equal sections (dressed spare, but picked out).

Ribs : Broad silver tinsel and twist.

Hackle: An Eagle's hackle (one side stripped) dyed yellow.

Throat : Widgeon.

II. *Whole-Feather Wings—continued :*

1. **Avon Eagle** (hook, 2 to 3 inches)—*continued :*

Wings : A pair of Golden Pheasant sword
feathers (back to back).

Sides : Jungle Cock ; two or three toppings
over.

2. **Benchill*** (hook, 1¼ to 3 inches).

Tag : Gold tinsel.

Tail : A topping, and the tip of a Golden
Pheasant's breast feather.

Butt : Black herl.

Body : Orange, scarlet, claret, and pale blue
Seal's fur (well picked out).

Ribs : Flat silver tinsel and twist.

Throat : A pale blue hackle.

Wings : A pair of tippets (back to back)
veiled with " married " strands (or, in large
sizes, narrow strips) of Peacock wing,
scarlet and blue Swan, Golden Pheasant
tail, and Bustard.

Cheeks : Strips of speckled Gallina wing and
Jungle Cock over ; a topping over all.

3. **Black Dose** (hook, 1¼ to 2 inches).

Tag : Silver thread and light orange floss.

Tail : A topping, and " married " narrow
strips of Teal and scarlet Swan (back to
back).

Body : Two or three turns of pale blue Seal's
fur, the rest black Seal's fur (left smooth).

Ribs : Oval silver tinsel.

Hackle : A black hackle.

* See Plate III.

II. *Whole-Feather Wings—continued :*

   3. **Black Dose** (hook, $1\frac{1}{4}$ to 2 inches)—*continued :*

      Throat : A light claret or fiery brown hackle.

      Wings : A pair of tippets (back to back) veiled with " married " strands of scarlet and green Swan, light mottled Turkey tail and Golden Pheasant tail; Peacock herl in strands above.

      Horns : Blue and yellow Macaw.

   4. **Black Ranger*** (hook, $1\frac{1}{4}$ to 2 inches).

      Tag : Silver thread and lemon floss.

      Tail : A topping and Indian Crow.

      Butt : Black herl.

      Body : Black floss.

      Ribs : Flat silver tinsel and twist.

      Hackle : A black hackle.

      Throat : A deep blue hackle.

      Wings : A pair of Jungle Cock feathers (back to back) covered for three-quarters of their length by two pairs of tippets (back to back), dressed in the manner indicated in Chap. X.

      Sides : Jungle Cock.

      Cheeks : Blue Chatterer ; a topping over.

      Horns : Blue and Yellow Macaw.

   5. **Candlestick Maker**† (hook, $\frac{3}{4}$ to $1\frac{1}{2}$ inches).

      Tag : Silver tinsel.

      Tail : A topping, scarlet Swan, and barred Summer Duck in strands.

    * See Plate V.   † See Plate I.

II. *Whole-Feather Wings—continued :*

5. **Candlestick Maker** * (hook, ¾ to 1½ inches)—
   continued :
   Body : First half, black floss ; second half,
   black Seal's fur.
   Ribs : Oval silver tinsel.
   Hackle : A fiery brown hackle.
   Throat : A black hackle.
   Wings : A pair of Jungle Cock feathers
   (back to back) ; three or four toppings
   over.

6. **Dandy** (hook, 1¼ to 2 inches).
   Tag : Silver thread and lemon floss.
   Tail : A topping, Jungle Cock and Blue
   Chatterer (the last somewhat shorter than
   the preceding).
   Butt : Black herl.
   Body : First two-thirds, flat silver tinsel ;
   remainder, pale blue floss.
   Ribs : Fine oval silver tinsel.
   Hackle : A pale blue hackle, beginning with
   the pale blue floss.
   Throat : Speckled Gallina.
   Wings : A pair of Jungle Cock feathers
   (back to back), and one pair of tippets
   dressed as in the Black Ranger above.
   Sides : Broad strips of barred Summer Duck,
   covering part of tippets up to bar nearest
   root.
   Cheeks : Blue Chatterer ; a topping over.
   Horns : Blue and Yellow Macaw.

* See Plate I.

II. *Whole-Feather Wings—continued* :

7. **Durham Ranger*** (hook, 1¼ to 2 inches).

    Tag : Silver tinsel.

    Tail : A topping and Indian Crow.

    Butt : Black herl.

    Body : Lemon floss, orange, fiery brown, and black Seal's fur in equal sections.

    Ribs : Flat silver tinsel and twist.

    Hackle : A badger hackle dyed yellow.

    Throat : A light blue hackle.

    Wings :
    Sides :
    Cheeks : } (As in Black Ranger.)
    Horns :

8. **Evening Star**† (hook, ¾ to 1½ inches).

    Tag : Silver thread and lemon floss.

    Tail : A topping.

    Body : Black Seal's fur (picked out towards the shoulder).

    Hackle : A black hackle.

    Throat : A deep blue hackle.

    Wings : Three pairs of Jungle Cock feathers (back to back), each pair shorter than the preceding ; four or five toppings over.

9. **Orange Parson*** (hook, 1¼ to 2 inches).

    Tag : Silver thread and lilac floss.

    Tail : A topping and tippet in strands.

    Body : Orange floss, orange, scarlet, and

---

    * See Plate I.   † See Plate V.

II. *Whole-Feather Wings—continued :*

9. **Orange Parson*** (hook, 1¼ to 2 inches) —
   continued :
   fiery brown Seal's fur in equal sections
   (picked out).

   Hackle : A lemon hackle.

   Throat : Cock of the Rock.

   Wings : A pair of tippets (back to back)
   veiled with Cock of the Rock.

   Sides : Barred Summer Duck strips.

   Cheeks : Blue Chatterer ; two or three top
   pings over.

   Horns : Blue and Yellow Macaw.

10. **Rosy Dawn*** (hook, 1¼ to 2 inches).

    Tag : Gold tinsel.

    Tail : A topping and tippet in strands.

    Butt : Black herl.

    Body : In two equal halves—first half, em-
    bossed silver tinsel ; second half, oval
    gold tinsel, butted at the joint with a
    magenta hackle.

    Throat : A magenta hackle, followed by a
    pale blue hackle.

    Wings : A pair of tippets (back to back),
    veiled with " married " strands of yellow,
    blue, and scarlet Swan and Golden
    Pheasant tail.

    Sides : Jungle Cock ; two or three toppings
    over.

    Horns : Blue and Scarlet Macaw.

* See Plate I.

II. *Whole-Feather Wings—continued :*

11. **Sir Herbert** (hook, 1¼ to 2 inches).

> Tag : Silver thread and pale orange floss.
> Tail : A topping and Indian Crow.
> Butt : Peacock sword feather.
> Body : First three-fourths, flat gold tinsel ; remainder, scarlet Seal's fur.
> Ribs : Fine oval silver tinsel.
> Hackle : A light orange hackle.
> Throat : A crimson hackle, or Golden Pheasant breast feather.
> Wings : A pair of tippets (back to back), veiled with " married " strands of Bustard, blue and crimson Swan, light mottled Turkey tail and Golden Pheasant tail ; strands of Peacock herl above.
> Sides : Jungle Cock ; a topping over.
> Horns : Scarlet Macaw.
> Head : Peacock herl.

12. **Stevenson** (hook, 1¼ to 2 inches).

> Tag : Silver thread and pale blue floss.
> Tail : A topping and Indian Crow.
> Butt : Black herl.
> Body : First quarter orange floss ; remainder, orange Seal's fur of a deeper shade.
> Ribs : Flat silver tinsel and silver twist.
> Hackle : A bright orange hackle.
> Throat : A pale blue hackle.
> Wings :
> Sides :
> Cheeks : } (As in Black Ranger.)
> Horns :

III. *Mixed-Wings :*

   1. **Baron** (hook, 1¼ to 2 inches).

          Tag : Silver thread and ruby red floss.

          Tail : A topping, Indian Crow and Blue Chatterer.

          Butt : Black herl.

          Body : In two equal halves—first half, flat silver tinsel, butted with black herl and veiled above and below with Indian Crow : second half, black floss.

          Ribs : Oval silver tinsel.

          Hackle : A dark claret hackle over the black floss.

          Throat : Jay.

          Wings : Mixed—tippet in strands ; "married" strands of scarlet, blue, and yellow Swan, Florican, Bustard, grey Turkey tail and Golden Pheasant tail ; "married" narrow strips of Teal and barred Summer Duck ; narrow strips of brown Mallard over.

          Sides : Jungle Cock.

          Cheeks : Blue Chatterer ; a topping over all.

          Horns : Blue and Yellow Macaw.

   2. **Black Doctor** * (hook, 1¼ to 2 inches).

          Tag : Silver thread and lemon floss.

          Tail : A topping and Indian Crow.

          Butt : Scarlet Berlin wool.

          Body : Black floss.

          Ribs : Oval silver tinsel.

          Hackle : A dark claret hackle.

          Throat : Speckled Gallina.

               * See Plate V.

III. *Mixed-Wings—continued :*

2. **Black Doctor** * (hook, 1¼ to 2 inches)—*continued :*
    Wings : Mixed—tippet in strands with strips
    of Golden Pheasant tail over ; " married "
    strands of scarlet, blue and yellow Swan,
    Florican, Bustard, Peacock wing, and
    light, mottled Turkey tail ; " married "
    narrow strips of Teal and barred Summer
    Duck ; narrow strips of brown Mallard
    over ; a topping over all.
    Head : Scarlet wool.

3. **Blue Doctor** (hook, 1¼ to 2 inches).
    Tag : Silver thread and golden yellow floss.
    Tail : A topping and tippet in strands.
    Butt : Scarlet Berlin wool.
    Body : Pale blue floss.
    Ribs : Oval silver tinsel.
    Hackle : A pale blue hackle.
    Throat : Jay.
    Wings : (As in Black Doctor, above.)
    Head : Scarlet wool.

4. **Childers** † (hook, 1¼ to 3 inches).
    Tag : Silver thread and pale blue floss.
    Tail : A topping and Indian Crow.
    Butt : Black herl.
    Body : Golden yellow floss, orange and fiery
    brown Seal's fur in equal sections.
    Ribs : Flat silver tinsel and twist.
    Hackle : A badger hackle dyed lemon.

* See Plate V.   † See Plate III.

III. *Mixed-Wings—continued :*

4. **Childers** * (hook, 1¼ to 3 inches)—*continued :*

Throat : Golden Pheasant breast feather, followed by Widgeon.

Wings : Mixed—a pair of Golden Pheasant breast feathers (back to back) ; " married " strands of scarlet, blue, orange and yellow Swan, Bustard, Florican, Golden Pheasant tail, cinnamon and mottled grey Turkey tail.

Sides : Barred Summer Duck strips.

Cheeks : Blue Chatterer ; a topping over all.

Horns : Blue and Yellow Macaw.

5. **Dunkeld** (hook, 1¼ to 2 inches).

Tag : Silver thread and light orange floss.

Tail : A topping, a pair of Jungle Cock feathers (back to back) veiled by a pair of Indian Crow feathers (back to back).

Butt : Black herl.

Body : Flat gold tinsel.

Ribs : Fine oval silver tinsel.

Hackle : A bright orange hackle.

Throat : Jay.

Wings : Mixed—tippet in strands ; " married " strands of scarlet, yellow, and blue Swan, Peacock wing, Bustard, Florican, Golden Pheasant tail and mottled brown Turkey tail ; strips of brown Mallard over.

Sides : Jungle Cock.

Cheeks : Blue Chatterer ; a topping over all.

Horns : Blue and Yellow Macaw.

* See Plate III.

III. *Mixed-Wings—continued* :

6. **Gordon** * (hook, $1\frac{1}{4}$ to 3 inches).

    Tag : Silver tinsel.

    Tail : A topping and Indian Crow.

    Butt : Black herl.

    Body : First quarter, light orange floss ; remainder, ruby red floss.

    Ribs : Flat silver tinsel and twist.

    Hackle : A claret hackle.

    Throat : A light blue hackle.

    Wings : Mixed—a pair of bright red hackles (back to back) or of Golden Pheasant sword feathers (in the larger sizes) ; strands of Peacock herl ; " married " strands of orange, scarlet, and blue Swan, Golden Pheasant tail, and Bustard.

    Cheeks : Tippets (small), and Jungle Cock over ; a topping over all.

    Horns : Blue and Yellow Macaw.

7. **Green Highlander** (hook, $1\frac{1}{4}$ to 2 inches) :

    Tag : Silver tinsel.

    Tail : A topping and barred Summer Duck in strands.

    Butt : Black herl.

    Body : First quarter, golden yellow floss ; remainder, bright green floss.

    Ribs : Oval silver tinsel.

    Hackle : A grass-green hackle.

    Throat : A lemon hackle.

    Wings : Mixed—tippet in strands ; " married " strands of yellow, orange, and green Swan,

* See Plate IV.

III. *Mixed-Wings—continued :*

7. **Green Highlander** (hook, 1¼ to 2 inches)—
     continued :
     Florican, Peacock wing and Golden
     Pheasant tail; "married" narrow strips
     of Teal and barred Summer Duck ; narrow
     strips of brown Mallard over.
     Sides : Jungle Cock.
     Cheeks : Indian Crow ; a topping over all.
     Horns : Blue and Yellow Macaw.

8. **Helmsdale Doctor** * (hook, 1¼ to 3 inches).
     Tag : Silver tinsel.
     Tail : A topping and tippet in strands.
     Butt : Scarlet Berlin wool.
     Body : Flat silver tinsel.
     Ribs : Fine oval tinsel.
     Throat : A lemon hackle.
     Wings : Mixed—Peacock herl in strands ;
     "married" strands of scarlet, blue, orange
     yellow, and white Swan, cinnamon and
     light mottled grey Turkey tail and
     Bustard ; a topping over all.
     Head : Scarlet Berlin wool.

9. **Kate** (hook, 1¼ to 2 inches).
     Tag : Silver thread and lemon floss.
     Tail : A topping and Blue Chatterer.
     Butt : Black herl.
     Body : Crimson floss.
     Ribs : Oval silver tinsel.
     Hackle : A crimson hackle.
     Throat : A lemon hackle.

* See Plate IV.

III. *Mixed-Wings—continued :*

9. **Kate** (hook, 1¼ to 2 inches)—*continued :*

Wings: Mixed—tippet in strands; "married" strands of scarlet and yellow Swan, Golden Pheasant tail and Bustard; "married" strips of Teal and barred Summer Duck; brown Mallard strips over.

Sides: Jungle Cock and Blue Chatterer; a topping over all.

Horns: Blue and Yellow Macaw.

10. **Mar Lodge** * (hook, 1¼ to 3 inches).

Tag: Silver tinsel.

Tail: A topping and a pair of Jungle Cock feathers (back to back).

Butt: Black herl.

Body: Fat silver tinsel, jointed at the middle with two or three turns of black floss.

Ribs: Narrow oval tinsel.

Throat: Speckled Gallina.

Wings: Mixed—tippet in strands; "married" strands of white Swan, Bustard, Florican, cinnamon, mottled grey and mottled brown Turkey tail and Golden Pheasant tail.

Sides: Broad strips of barred Summer Duck.

Cheeks: Jungle Cock; a topping over all.

Horns: Blue and Yellow Macaw.

11. **Popham** † (hook, 1¼ to 2 inches).

Tag: Silver Tinsel.

Tail: A topping and Indian Crow.

Butt: Black herl.

* See Plate V.   † See Plate I.

III. *Mixed-Wings—continued :*

11. **Popham** * (hook, 1¼ to 2 inches)—*continued :*

Body : In three equal sections, of orange, lemon yellow, and pale blue floss respectively ; the first and second sections each butted with black herl, and all sections veiled above and below with Indian Crow.

Ribs : Oval gold tinsel for first and second sections, oval silver tinsel for third section.

Throat : Jay.

Wings : Mixed—tippet in strands ; "married" strands of Bustard, Florican, Peacock wing, scarlet, blue, orange, and yellow Swan, and Golden Pheasant tail ; Peacock sword over.

Sides : Barred Summer Duck (a rather broad strip) ; two or three toppings over all.

Horns : Blue and Yellow Macaw.

12. **Sherbrook** (hook, 1 to 1¼ inches).

Tag : Silver thread and lemon floss.

Tail : A topping and Indian Crow.

Body : First third, pale orange floss ; remainder, pale blue floss.

Ribs : Oval silver tinsel.

Throat : A pale blue hackle.

Wings : Mixed—tippet in strands ; "married" strands of yellow, white, orange, crimson, and blue Swan, Golden Pheasant tail, Florican and Peacock wing ; "married" narrow strips of barred Summer Duck and Pintail ; narrow strips of brown Mallard over ; a topping over all.

Horns : Blue and Yellow Macaw.

* See Plate I.

III. *Mixed-Wings—continued :*

13. **Silver Doctor*** (hook, 1¼ to 3 inches).

   Tag : Silver thread and golden yellow floss.
   Tail : A topping and Blue Chatterer.
   Butt : Scarlet Berlin wool.
   Body : Flat silver tinsel.
   Ribs : Fine oval silver tinsel.
   Throat : A pale blue hackle, followed by Widgeon.
   Wings : (As in Blue Doctor.)
   Head : Scarlet Berlin wool.

14. **Silver Grey** † (hook, 1¼ to 3 inches).

   Tag : Silver thread and golden yellow floss.
   Tail : A topping and barred Summer Duck (in strands).
   Butt : Black herl.
   Body : Flat silver tinsel.
   Ribs : Fine oval silver tinsel.
   Hackle : A badger hackle.
   Throat : Widgeon.
   Wings : Mixed—tippet in strands ; "married" strands of white, yellow, and green Swan, Bustard, Florican, and Golden Pheasant tail ; "married" strips of Pintail and barred Summer Duck ; brown Mallard strips over.
   Cheeks : Jungle Cock ; a topping over all.
   Horns : Blue and Yellow Macaw.

15. **Silver Wilkinson** (hook, 1¼ to 3 inches).

   To all intents and purposes this is the same fly as the Silver Doctor, except that the

   * See Plate IV.   † See Plate I.

III. *Mixed-Wings—continued :*

15. **Silver Wilkinson** (hook, 1¼ to 3 inches)—
    continued :

    throat is a magenta hackle instead of a
    blue hackle, followed by Widgeon ; the
    scarlet wool for the head is omitted, and
    sometimes Indian Crow as well as Chatterer
    figures in the tail, and cheeks of Indian
    Crow and Chatterer are added. (As is the
    case with many patterns, however, no two
    people dress the Silver Wilkinson alike.)

16. **Sir Richard** * (hook, 1¼ to 3 inches).
    Tag : Silver thread and dark orange floss.
    Tail : A topping and Indian Crow.
    Butt : Black herl.
    Body : Black floss.
    Ribs : Flat silver tinsel and twist.
    Hackle : A black hackle (black Heron in
      the bigger sizes).
    Throat : Speckled Gallina.
    Wings : Mixed—" married " strands of scar-
      let, orange, and blue Swan, Bustard,
      Florican, mottled grey Turkey tail, and
      Golden Pheasant tail ; a short strip of
      Speckled Gallina wing over.
    Cheeks : Blue Chatterer ; a topping over all.
    Horns : Blue and Yellow Macaw.

IV. *Built-Wings :*

1. **Butcher** † (hook, 1¼ to 2 inches).
    Tag : Silver thread and lemon floss.
    Tail : A topping and Blue Chatterer.

    * See Plate III.   † See Plate I.

IV. *Built-Wings—continued :*

1. **Butcher*** (hook, 1¼ to 2 inches)—*continued :*

   Butt : Black herl.

   Body : Fiery brown, pale blue, claret, and dark blue Seal's fur in equal sections (picked out).

   Ribs : Flat silver tinsel and twist.

   Hackle : A dark claret or black hackle.

   Throat : A lemon hackle followed by Speckled Gallina.

   Wings : A pair of tippets (back to back), covered by a pair of Golden Pheasant breast feathers, and these by a pair of broad strips of Teal ; "married" narrow strips of yellow Swan and Bustard, scarlet and blue Swan, orange Swan, and Golden Pheasant tail ; strips of brown Mallard over (rather broad).

   Cheeks : Blue Chatterer ; a topping over all (sometimes there is no topping).

   Horns : Blue and Yellow Macaw.

2. **Dusty Miller** † (hook, 1¼ to 3 inches).

   Tag : Silver thread and golden yellow floss.

   Tail : A topping and Indian Crow.

   Butt : Black herl.

   Body : First two-thirds, embossed silver tinsel ; remainder, orange floss.

   Ribs : Fine oval silver tinsel.

   Hackle : A golden olive hackle over the orange floss only (sometimes the hackle is omitted).

---

* See Plate I.   † See Plate V.

IV. *Built-Wings—continued :*

2. **Dusty Miller*** (hook, 1¼ to 3 inches)—*continued:*

Throat : Speckled Gallina.

Wings : A pair of black white-tipped Turkey tail strips (back to back) ; over these, but not entirely hiding them, a mixed " sheath " of " married " strands of Teal, yellow, scarlet, and orange Swan, Bustard, Florican, and Golden Pheasant tail ; " married " narrow strips of Pintail and barred Summer Duck ; narrow strips of brown Mallard over.

Cheeks : Jungle Cock ; a topping over all.

Horns : Blue and Yellow Macaw.

3. **Greenwell** (hook, 1¼ to 2 inches).

Tag : Silver tinsel.

Tail : A topping and a pair of Jungle Cock feathers (back to back).

Butt : Black herl.

Body : Pale blue floss.

Ribs : Broad flat silver tinsel and twist.

Hackle : A pale blue hackle.

Throat : Widgeon.

Wings : (As in Dusty Miller, except that the scarlet and orange Swan in the mixed " sheaths " is replaced by blue Swan.)

Cheeks : Jungle Cock ; a topping over.

Horns : Blue and Yellow Macaw.

4. **Jock Scott**† (hook, 1¼ to 3 inches).

Tag : Silver tinsel.

Tail : A topping and Indian Crow.

* See Plate V.   † See Plate I.

IV. *Built-Wings —continued :*

4. **Jock Scott** * (hook, $1\frac{1}{4}$ to 3 inches)—*continued :*

Butt : Black herl.

Body : In two equal halves—first half, golden yellow floss butted with black herl, and veiled above and below with six or more Toucan feathers ; second half, black floss.

Ribs : Fine oval silver tinsel over golden yellow floss, broader oval silver tinsel or flat silver tinsel and twist (in the large sizes) over the black floss.

Hackle : A black hackle over the black floss.

Throat : Speckled Gallina.

Wings : A pair of black white-tipped Turkey tail strips (back to back) ; over these, but not entirely covering them, a " mixed " sheath of " married " strands of Peacock wing, yellow, scarlet, and blue Swan, Bustard, Florican, and Golden Pheasant tail ; two strands of Peacock sword feather above ; " married " narrow strips of Teal and barred Summer Duck at the sides ; brown Mallard over.

Sides : Jungle Cock.

Cheeks : Blue Chatterer ; a topping over all.

Horns : Blue and Yellow Macaw.

5. **Red Sandy** (hook, $1\frac{1}{4}$ to 3 inches).

Tag : Silver thread and golden yellow floss.

Tail : A topping, Indian Crow and Blue Chatterer over.

Butt : Scarlet Berlin wool.

Body : Flat silver tinsel.

* See Plate I.

IV. *Built-Wings—continued :*

5. **Red Sandy** (hook, 1¼ to 3 inches)—*continued :*

Ribs : Fine oval silver tinsel.

Hackle : A badger hackle dyed deep orange.

Throat : Jay, or Speckled Gallina dyed blue in the larger sizes.

Wings :
Sides :
Cheeks : { (As in Jock Scott precisely, except that the blue Swan is omitted from the mixed " sheath," and there is the addition of Indian Crow under the Blue Chatterer cheeks.)

Horns : Blue and Scarlet Macaw.

Head : Scarlet Berlin wool.

6. **Torrish** * (hook, 1¼ to 3 inches).

Tag : Silver thread and golden yellow floss.

Tail : A topping and tippet in strands.

Butt : Black herl.

Body : Oval silver tinsel, butted at the junction of the first two-fifths with the subsequent three-fifths with black herl and veiled above and below with Indian Crow.

Ribs : Fine oval silver tinsel over the anterior three-fifths of the body.

Hackle : A lemon hackle (with the ribs).

Throat : A deep orange hackle.

Wings :
Cheeks : { (As in Dusty Miller, with the addition of Indian Crow over
Horns : the Jungle Cock cheeks.)

* See Plate V.

V. *Herl-Wings :*

   1. **Alexandra** (hook, $\frac{3}{4}$ to $1\frac{1}{8}$ inches).
        Tail : Scarlet Ibis.
        Body : Flat silver tinsel.
        Throat : A black or badger hackle.
        Wings : Peacock sword feather in strips.
        Cheeks : Jungle Cock.

   2. **Beauly Snow Fly*** (hook, $1\frac{1}{2}$ to 3 inches).
        Body : Pale blue Seal's fur (dressed sparely).
        Ribs : Broad, flat, silver tinsel and gold
          twist.
        Hackle : A black Heron's hackle from third
          turn of tinsel.
        Wings : Peacock herl in strands.
        Head : Orange Seal's fur.

   3. **Green Peacock** † (hook, $\frac{3}{4}$ to $1\frac{1}{8}$ inches).
        Tag : Silver thread and golden yellow
          floss.
        Tail : A topping.
        Body : Pale blue floss.
        Ribs : Oval silver tinsel.
        Throat : A pale blue hackle.
        Wings : Peacock sword feather in strips.

VI. *Topping-Wings :*

   1. **Black Prince** ‡ (hook, $\frac{3}{4}$ to $1\frac{1}{2}$ inches).
        Tag : Silver tinsel.
        Tail : A topping and Jungle Cock.
        Butt : Black herl.

     * See Plate VII.   † See Plate IX.
              ‡ See Plate V.

VI. *Topping-Wings—continued :*

1. **Black Prince** * (hook, $\frac{3}{4}$ to $1\frac{1}{2}$ inches)—*continued :*

Body : Flat silver tinsel in three joints, each joint butted with black herl and veiled above and below with the small black feather from the back of the head and neck of the Indian Crow, or (almost as good) the greenish-bronze feather from the corresponding part of the common English cock Pheasant.

Throat : A black hackle.

Wings : Six (or more) toppings.

Horns : Blue and Yellow Macaw.

2. **Canary** * (hook, $\frac{3}{4}$ to $1\frac{1}{2}$ inches).

Tag : Gold tinsel.

Tail : A topping and Indian Crow.

Body : Flat silver tinsel in two joints, each joint butted with black herl, and veiled above and below with three or more Toucan feathers.

Throat : Cock of the Rock.

Wings : Six (or more) toppings.

Horns : Scarlet Macaw.

3. **Variegated Sun Fly** † (hook, $\frac{3}{4}$ to $1\frac{1}{8}$ inches).

Tag : Silver thread and pale blue floss.

Tail : A topping and Cock of the Rock (in strands).

Body : Black, yellow and orange Berlin wool wound round together.

Throat : A black hackle.

Wings : Six (or more) toppings.

* See Plate V.   † See Plate IX.

1. **Akroyd** * (hook, $1\frac{1}{2}$ to 3 inches).

Tag : Silver tinsel.

Tail : A topping and tippet in strands.

Body : First half, light orange Seal's fur ; second half, black floss.

Ribs : Oval silver tinsel over the orange Seal's fur ; flat silver tinsel and twist over black floss.

Hackle : A lemon hackle over the orange Seal's fur ; a black Heron's hackle over the black floss.

Throat : Teal

Wings : A pair of cinnamon Turkey tail strips (set flat) White Turkey tail strips are often used, as in Plate VI., in which case the pattern is known as the white-winged Akroyd.

Cheeks : Jungle Cock (drooping).

2. **Dunt** (hook, $1\frac{1}{2}$ to 3 inches).

Tag : Silver thread and pale blue floss.

Tail : A topping and a pair of Jungle Cock feathers (back to back).

Body : Yellow, orange and fiery brown Seal's fur in equal sections (dressed thin, but well picked out).

Ribs : Flat silver tinsel and twist.

Hackle : A black Heron's hackle from third turn of tinsel.

Throat : Teal.

Wings : A pair of brown Turkey tail strips, with black bars and white tips (set flat).

Cheeks : Jungle Cock (drooping).

* See Plate VI.

3. **Gardener** (hook, 1½ to 3 inches).

    Tag : Gold thread and crimson floss.

    Tail : A topping and tippet in strands.

    Body : Yellow, green and dark blue Seal's fur, in equal sections (dressed thin, but well picked out).

    Ribs : Flat silver tinsel and twist.

    Hackle : A pale orange hackle.

    Throat : A black Heron's hackle.

    Wings : (As in Akroyd.)

    Cheeks : Jungle Cock (drooping).

4. **Glentana** * (hook, 1½ to 3 inches).

    Tag : Silver thread and lemon floss.

    Tail : A topping and the tip of a Golden Pheasant's breast feather.

    Body : First third, light orange Seal's fur ; remainder, claret Seal's fur (dressed thin, but well picked out).

    Ribs : Flat silver tinsel and twist.

    Hackle : A black Heron's hackle from third turn of tinsel.

    Throat : Widgeon.

    Wings : (As in Akroyd.)

5. **Grey Eagle** * (hook, 2 to 3 inches).

    Tag : Silver tinsel.

    Tail : (As in Glentana.)

    Body : Light orange, deep orange, scarlet and pale blue Seal's fur in equal sections (dressed thin, but well picked out).

    Ribs : Flat silver tinsel and twist.

    Hackle : An Eagle's hackle (one side stripped) from third turn of tinsel.

* See Plate VI.

5. **Grey Eagle*** (hook, 2 to 3 inches)—*continued :*

Throat: Widgeon.

Wings: A pair of light, mottled grey Turkey tail strips (set flat).

6. **Jock o' Dee*** (hook, 1½ to 3 inches).

Tag: Silver tinsel.

Tail: A topping and Indian Crow.

Body: Two-fifths, lemon floss; remainder, black floss.

Ribs: Flat silver tinsel and twist.

Hackle: A grey Heron's hackle from third turn of tinsel.

Throat: Widgeon.

Wings: (As in Akroyd.)

7. **Moonlight** (hook, 1½ to 3 inches).

Tag: Silver tinsel.

Tail: A topping and a pair of Jungle Cock feathers (back to back).

Body: In two equal halves—first half, silver tinsel, veiled above and below with a pair (or two pairs) of Blue Chatterer feathers (back to back); second half, black floss.

Ribs: Fine oval silver tinsel over flat silver tinsel; broader oval gold tinsel over black floss.

Hackle: A black Heron's hackle over black floss

Throat: Speckled Gallina.

Wings: (As in Akroyd.)

8. **Tricolor** (hook, 1½ to 3 inches).

Tag: Silver tinsel.

Tail: A topping and the tip of a Golden Pheasant's breast feather.

* See Plate VI.

8. **Tricolor** (hook, 1½ to 3 inches)—*continued :*

> Body : Pale yellow, light blue and scarlet Seal's
> fur in equal sections.
>
> Ribs : Flat silver tinsel and twist.
>
> Hackle : A grey Heron's hackle from third turn
> of tinsel.
>
> Throat : Teal.
>
> Wings : (As in Akroyd.)

9. **Yellow Eagle** (hook, 2 to 3 inches).

> This pattern is the same as the Avon Eagle
> (*q.v.*), except for the wings, which are similar
> to those of the Grey Eagle above.

(C) SPEY FLIES.

1. **Black King** (hook, 1½ to 2½ inches).

> Body : Black floss.
>
> Ribs : Flat and oval silver tinsels and silver
> thread.
>
> Hackle : A bronze-black Spey-cock's hackle.
>
> Throat : Teal.
>
> Wings : Brown Mallard strips (short).

2. **Carron** * (hook, 1½ to 2½ inches).

> Body : Orange Berlin wool.
>
> Ribs : Flat silver tinsel, scarlet floss, and silver
> thread.
>
> Hackle : A black Heron's hackle (from the
> fourth turn of tinsel).
>
> Throat : Teal.
>
> Wings : (As in Black King.)

* See Plate VII.

3. **Gold Riach** (hook, $1\frac{1}{2}$ to $2\frac{1}{2}$ inches).

> Body : First quarter, orange Berlin wool ; remainder, black Berlin wool.
>
> Ribs : Flat gold tinsel, oval gold tinsel, and silver thread.
>
> Hackle : A reddish-brown Spey-cock's hackle.
>
> Throat : Widgeon.
>
> Wings : (As in Black King.)

4. **Green King*** (hook, $1\frac{1}{2}$ to $2\frac{1}{2}$ inches).

> Body : Green Berlin wool.
>
> Ribs : Flat gold and silver tinsels and gold thread.
>
> Throat : Widgeon.
>
> Wings : (As in Black King.)

5. **Grey Heron *** (hook, $1\frac{1}{2}$ to $2\frac{1}{2}$ inches).

> Body : First third, lemon Berlin wool ; remainder, black Berlin wool.
>
> Ribs : Flat silver tinsel, and oval silver and gold tinsels.
>
> Hackle : A grey Heron hackle from one end of body tied in at the point (or, almost better, as in the fly figured on Plate VII., a hackle from the rump of a Blue Game hen).
>
> Throat : Speckled Gallina.
>
> Wings : (As in Black King.)

6. **Lady Caroline** (hook, $1\frac{1}{2}$ to $2\frac{1}{2}$ inches).

> Tail : Golden Pheasant breast feathers in strands.
>
> Body : Olive green and light brown Berlin wools wound together in the proportion of two strands of the latter to one of the former.

* See Plate VII.

6. **Lady Caroline** (hook, 1½ to 2½ inches)—*continued :*

   Ribs : Flat gold tinsel, and oval silver and gold tinsels.

   Hackle : A grey Heron hackle—as in the preceding pattern.

   Throat : Golden Pheasant breast feather.

   Wings : (As in Black King.)

7. **Purple King** * (hook, 1½ to 2½ inches).

   Body : Purple Berlin wool.

   Ribs : Flat gold tinsel, lilac floss, and gold thread.

   Hackle : A bronze-black Spey-cock's hackle.

   Throat : Teal.

   Wings : (As in Black King.)

(D) Grubs.

1. **Brown Shrimp** (hook, ¾ to 1¼ inches).

   Tag : Gold tinsel.

   Tail : The tip of a Golden Pheasant's breast feather and a pair of Jungle Cock's feathers (back to back).

   Butt : A golden Pheasant's breast feather, followed by a freckled brown Partridge neck feather—used as hackles.

   Body : In two equal halves—fur from a Hare's face butted in the middle in the same way and with similar feathers as for the butt, the feathers, however, to be a bit longer.

   Throat : The same as in the two butts, feathers to be longer still.

   * See Plate VII.

2. **Glow-worm** * (hook, $\frac{3}{4}$ to $1\frac{1}{4}$ inches).

> Tag : Silver tinsel.
>
> Tail : A tuft of scarlet Berlin wool.
>
> Butt : A cochybondu hackle.
>
> Body : In two equal halves of oval gold tinsel, tightly twisted round before being wound on, butted at the joint with a cochybondhu hackle, somewhat longer in the fibre than the previous hackle.
>
> Throat : A cochybondhu hackle—longer still in the fibre.

3. **Grey Palmer** (hook, $\frac{3}{4}$ to $1\frac{1}{4}$ inches).

> Tag : Silver tinsel.
>
> Body : Peacock herl.
>
> Ribs : Flat silver tinsel, comparatively broad.
>
> Hackle : A grizzled hackle from a Plymouth Rock hen, from the *first* turn of tinsel.

4. **Jungle Hornet** † (hook, $1\frac{1}{4}$ to $1\frac{3}{4}$ inches).

> Tag : Silver tinsel.
>
> Tail : Scarlet Ibis in strands and a pair of Jungle Cock feathers (back to back).
>
> Butt : A cochybondhu hackle.
>
> Body : In two equal halves, each of an equal number of turns of yellow and black Berlin wools wound together, and each butted at the joint with a cochybondhu hackle and veiled above with a pair of Jungle Cock feathers (back to back).
>
> Throat : A cochybondhu hackle. (Each succeeding cochybondhu hackle to be larger in the fibre than the preceding one.)

---

* See Plate IX. † See Plate VII.

5. **Silver Partridge** * (hook, $\frac{3}{4}$ to $1\frac{1}{8}$ inches).

    Tail : The tip of a Golden Pheasant's breast feather.

    Body : Flat silver tinsel.

    Ribs : Fine oval silver tinsel.

    Hackle : A grizzled hackle.

    Throat : A freckled brown Partridge hackle.

6. **Spring Grub** (hook, 1 to $1\frac{3}{4}$ inches).

    Tag : Silver thread and pale blue floss.

    Tail : " Married " narrow strips of scarlet Ibis and blue and Yellow Macaw (back to back).

    Butt : A badger hackle dyed orange.

    Body : In two equal halves—first half, golden yellow floss ; second half-black floss, butted at the joint with pale Blue Game hen's hackle or (when procurable) a natural blue Gallina hackle.

    Ribs : Black Berlin wool over the yellow floss, oval silver tinsel over the black floss.

    Throat : A cochybondhu hackle, followed by a richly coloured speckled Grouse hackle.

7. **Tippet Grub** † (hook, 1 to $1\frac{3}{4}$ inches).

    Tag : Gold tinsel and scarlet Seal's fur.

    Butt : A tippet (wound as a hackle) followed by a furnace hackle.

    Body : In two equal halves, each beginning with three turns of silver thread, followed by green Berlin wool, butted at the joint with similar feathers and in the same way as for the butt.

    Throat : As for the butts (larger fibred feathers).

    Head : Silver thread.

        * See Plate IX.   † See Plate VII.

1. **Black Goldfinch*** (hook, 1 to $1\frac{3}{4}$ inches).

  Tag : Silver thread and deep orange silk.

  Tail : A topping and Indian Crow.

  Butt : Black herl.

  Body : Black floss.

  Ribs : Oval gold tinsel.

  Hackle : A golden olive hackle.

  Throat : Jay.

  Wings : Tippet in strands, covered by strips of orange Swan (set upright).

  Cheeks : Indian Crow ; two or three toppings over all.

  Horns : Blue and Yellow Macaw.

2. **Blue Palmer** (hook, 1 to $1\frac{3}{4}$ inches).

  Tag : Gold tinsel.

  Tail : A topping and tippet in strands.

  Butt : Black herl.

  Body : Deep blue floss.

  Ribs : Oval gold tinsel.

  Hackle : Jay.

  Throat : Jay.

  Wings : Mixed—tippet in strands ; "married" strands of scarlet, blue, yellow, and orange Swan, Florican, Bustard, Golden Pheasant tail ; "married" narrow strips of Teal (or Pintail) and barred Summer Duck ; strips (rather broad) of brown Mallard over.

  Horns : Blue and Yellow Macaw.

  Head : Black herl.

* See Plate VIII.

3. **Claret Jay*** (hook, 1 to 1¾ inches).

    Tag : Silver thread and deep orange floss.

    Tail : A topping, Cock of the Rock and tippet in strands.

    Body : First three-quarters, deep claret Seal's fur ; remainder, purple Seal's fur.

    Ribs : Oval gold tinsel.

    Hackle : A deep claret hackle.

    Throat : Jay.

    Wings : ⎫

    Horns : ⎬ (As in Blue Palmer.)

    Head : ⎭

4. **Fenian** (hook, 1 to 1¾ inches).

    Tag : Silver tinsel.

    Tail : A topping and Blue Chatterer.

    Body : First quarter, bright orange Seal's fur ; remainder, bright green Seal's fur.

    Ribs : Oval gold tinsel.

    Hackle : A golden olive hackle over the green Seal's fur.

    Throat : Jay.

    Wings : Mixed—tippet in strands ; " married " strands of green, yellow, and orange Swan, Florican and Golden Pheasant tail ; " married " narrow strips of Pintail and barred Summer Duck ; brown Mallard strips over.

    Head : Black herl.

5. **Fiery Brown*** (hook, 1 to 1¾ inches).

    Tag : Silver thread and golden yellow floss.

    Tail : A topping and tippet in strands.

    Body : First quarter, bright orange Seal's fur ;

* See Plate VIII.

5. **Fiery Brown** * (hook, 1 to 1¾ inches)—*continued :*
   second quarter, light blue Seal's fur; remainder,
   fiery brown Seal's fur.

   Ribs : Oval silver tinsel.

   Hackle : A fiery brown hackle over the blue and
   fiery brown Seal's fur.

   Throat : Jay.

   Wings : ⎫
   Head : ⎭ (As in Blue Palmer.)

6. **Half Grey and Brown** * (hook, 1¼ to 2 inches).
   Tag : Silver thread and light orange floss.

   Tail : A topping and the tip of a Golden
   Pheasant's breast feather.

   Body : First half, grey Seal's fur (or grey Squirrel);
   second half, fiery brown Seal's fur.

   Ribs : Oval silver tinsel.

   Hackle : A grizzled hackle.

   Throat : A fiery brown hackle, followed by a
   lemon hackle.

   Wings : Mixed—tippet in strands; "married"
   strands of orange, yellow, and scarlet Swan,
   Pintail and Golden Pheasant tail ; brown
   Mallard strips over.

   Head : Black herl.

7. **Half Yellow and Black*** (hook, 1 to 1¾ inches).
   Tag : Silver tinsel.

   Tail : A topping and Indian Crow.

   Butt : Black herl.

   Body : First half, golden yellow floss ; second half,
   black floss.

   Ribs : Oval gold tinsel.

* See Plate VIII.

7. **Half Yellow and Black** * (hook, 1 to 1¾ inches)—
   continued :

   Hackle : A dark claret hackle over black floss.

   Throat : Jay.

   Wings : Mixed — tippet in strands ; " married "
   strands of scarlet, yellow, and orange Swan,
   Bustard, and Golden Pheasant tail ; brown
   Mallard strips over.

   Horns : Blue and yellow Macaw.

   Head : Black herl.

8. **Goldfinch** (hook, 1 to 1¾ inches).

   This pattern is exactly similar to the Black Goldfinch except for the body, which is either of
   light orange floss or flat gold tinsel.

9. **Golden Olive** * (hook, 1 to 1¼ inches).

   Tag : Silver thread and golden yellow floss.

   Tail : A topping, Cock of the Rock and tippet in
   strands.

   Body : Light orange, bright orange, fiery brown,
   and olive brown Seal's fur in equal sections.

   Ribs : Oval gold tinsel.

   Hackle : A golden olive hackle.

   Throat : Jay.

   Wings : ⎫
   Horns : ⎬ (As in Blue Palmer, except that green
   Head : ⎭ Swan is added to the wing.)

10. **Grouse and Green** † (hook, 1 to 1¾ inches).

    Tag : Silver tinsel.

    Tail : A topping.

    Butt : Black herl.

    Body : Grass-green floss.

    * See Plate VIII.   † See Plate IX.

10. **Grouse and Green*** (hook, 1 to 1¾ inches)—
    continued :

    Ribs : Oval silver tinsel.

    Hackle : A speckled feather from the rump of
    a cock Grouse (one side stripped) from third
    turn of tinsel.

    Throat : (Same as hackle.)

    Wings : Mixed – tippet in strands ; "married"
    strands of yellow, green, scarlet, and blue
    Swan, Florican and Golden Pheasant tail ;
    strips of brown Mallard over.

    Head : Black herl.

11. **Grouse and Orange** (hook, 1 to 1¾ inches).

    Tag : Silver tinsel.

    Tail : A topping and Indian Crow.

    Butt : Black herl.

    Body : First quarter, pale blue floss ; remainder,
    bright orange floss.

    Ribs : Oval gold tinsel.

    Hackle : ⎫
    Throat : ⎭ (As in Grouse and Green.)

    Wings : Tippet in strands, veiled by Golden
    Pheasant breast feather in strands ; broad
    strips of speckled Gallina wing ; strips of
    brown Mallard over.

    Horns : Blue and Yellow Macaw.

    Head : Black herl.

12. **Lemon and Blue** † (hook, 1¼ to 2 inches).

    Tag : Silver thread and deep orange floss.

    Tail : A topping and tippet in strands.

    Butt : Black herl.

* See Plate IX.   † See Plate VIII.

12. **Lemon and Blue** * (hook, $1\frac{1}{4}$ to 2 inches)—*continued :*

    Body : Deep blue Seal's fur.

    Ribs : Oval silver tinsel.

    Hackle : A blue hackle.

    Throat : A lemon hackle.

    Wings : ⎫

    Horns : ⎬ (As in Blue Palmer.)

    Head : ⎭

13. **Lemon and Grey** * (hook, $1\frac{1}{4}$ to 2 inches).

    Tag : Silver thread and golden yellow floss.

    Tail : A topping and Indian Crow.

    Butt : Black herl.

    Body : Grey Seal's fur (or Grey Squirrel or Silver Monkey).

    Ribs : Oval silver tinsel.

    Hackle : A grizzled hackle.

    Throat : A lemon hackle.

    Wings : Mixed—tippet in strands ; " married " strands of green, yellow, and orange Swan, Bustard, Florican, Golden Pheasant tail ; " married " narrow strands of Teal and barred Summer Duck ; brown Mallard strips over.

    Head : Black herl.

14. **Orange and Grey** (hook, $1\frac{1}{4}$ to 2 inches).

    Tag : Silver thread and golden yellow floss.

    Tail : A topping, Indian Crow and Blue Chatterer.

    Body : First third, bright orange floss ; remainder, grey Seal's fur (or grey Squirrel or Silver Monkey).

    Ribs : Fine oval gold tinsel over orange floss, oval silver tinsel over remainder of body.

* See Plate VIII.

14. **Orange and Grey** (hook, $1\frac{1}{4}$ to 2 inches)—*continued :*

Hackle : An orange hackle over orange floss, a
grizzled hackle over rest of body.

Throat : A lemon hackle.

Wings : ⎫
Horns : ⎬ (As in Blue Palmer.)
Head : ⎭

15. **Thunder and Lightning** (Irish)* (hook, 1 to $1\frac{3}{4}$
inches).

Tag : Silver thread and golden yellow floss.

Tail : A topping and Indian Crow.

Butt : Black herl.

Body : Black floss.

Ribs : Oval silver tinsel.

Hackle : A fiery brown hackle.

Throat : Jay.

Wings : Mixed—" married " strands of yellow,
scarlet, and blue Swan, Bustard and Golden
Pheasant tail ; strips of brown Mallard over.

Horns : Blue and Yellow Macaw.

Head : Black herl.

* See Plate VIII.

PART TWO

By John Veniard

INTRODUCTION

One of the interesting features of angling literature during the early 1970s has been the re-introduction of classical works, presented either in facsimile form or modern format. Speaking for myself, I think this is a very good sign, for not only does it give present generations of anglers an opportunity to study the works of the masters who laid down the foundations of our angling as practised today, it also gives them the chance to observe the painstaking efforts that went into their experiments and observations.

There must be many young anglers today who think that most of the flies they use and the techniques of their presentation, are the result of contemporary thought, but perusal of these re-introduced works will soon prove that this is not always the case.

Admittedly modern production methods have brought new innovations as far as our main tackle is concerned, but I am thinking more about our terminal tackle in this discourse.

Modern tackle has made possible the shooting head line and the double haul technique, but the lure they take such great distances today, had its beginnings in the "Demons" and "Terrors" that were in use regularly at the turn of this century.

One of the most popular flies today is the Nymph, tied and fished in many variations, and during the last ten years tens of thousands of words must have been written on its potentialities. It was G. E. M. Skues, however, who first saw the potential of this type of fishing, and his initial book on the nymph and how to present it, appeared in 1910!

I maintain, therefore, that one can do far worse than return to the origins of our sport and interest, and also that those publishers of today who are making this possible, should be deserving of our thanks.

Probably the biggest change that has taken place in fly fishing, is that of the angler's approach to the artificial fly. This has been brought about by the change in the fly fishermans' habits, in that he now considers that the fly one ties oneself must be superior to that which is shop bought. This does not mean that the amateur ties a better fly than the professional fly tyer, and this is best explained, I think, in the last paragraph in Donald Overfield's appreciation of Pryce-Tannatt at the beginning of this book. Fortunately, many professional tyers are also expert anglers, so those who do not have the opportunity of tying their own flies can still buy with some confidence. I made some attempt to describe the vital difference between the shop bought fly and one of one's own tying, in "Fly Tying Development and Progress", and it is my considered opinion that the fly has now progressed from the stage when it was usually a shop bought item of tackle, to that of an expression of an individual angler's interpretation of a dressing which will take fish, plus an essential part of his angling pleasure. The degree to which he indulges in this pleasure is plainly manifested in the contents of countless fly boxes which are so often produced with concealed (but nonetheless obvious) pride, and the many serious terms in which various items of material and their application are discussed.

I do not think that this aspect of the fly tying craft was really appreciated when Pryce-Tannatt produced his book, although the obvious beauty of all the flies in the illustrations must have done much to foster this interest in the merits of a fly for its appearance only.

You may have observed that I referred to fly tying as a "craft" rather than as an "art" which is its customary description. I do this deliberately because I know that fly tying can be practised by anyone who is interested enough, whereas an artist has a special "gift". That the craft can be transformed into an art form is also true however, and I have been fortunate enough to have seen many examples where this has been the case, and I feel sure that readers will agree with me that this applies to all the flies illustrated in this book.

There is one instance where Pryce-Tannatt makes a contribution to fostering pride in the appearance of one's flies, and that is in the section devoted to giving "form" and symmetry to one's efforts. I know that as far as I am concerned, this prompted me to make my own flies as attractive as possible, and resulted in my tying flies that were worth looking at, as well as being used to catch fish.

When "How to Dress Salmon Flies" was written, the warehouses of London were stuffed with the plumages required by the millinery trade of that era, and it was from this source that all the exotic feathers listed in his dressings were procured. We all know now that this source has practically dried up, not only because fashions have changed, but also because of belated conservation schemes which now rightly protect the original possessors of these beautiful appendages.

The latest of these of course, is the Jungle Fowl, whose hackles supplied the "eyes", "shoulders" or "cheeks" of so many patterns, many of which are so beautifully illustrated in this book. However, human ingenuity has made some attempt to replace this item, although in my experience there does not seem to have been much diminution in the sizes of catches which could be attributed to using flies not having the original feather, or its substitute.

This brings me to my main theme, and one of the reasons why I was very pleased to assist with the re-introduction of this book.

In my particular position in the Fishing Tackle world, I have been able to observe the very many changes which have taken place in salmon fly design, and also watch with regret, the decline of the "exotic" fly and its replacement with the hair winged variety and the tube fly. Please remember that I am discussing the aesthetic merits of the fly now, not its fish-taking ability.

As many plumages became unobtainable, either by protection or scarcity, substitutes had to be sought, and in this trend it was found that hair was not only cheaper and more readily available, it also took fish, a most important factor as salmon fishing became more expensive and difficult to get. So began the decline of the "exotic" fly, but I am hoping that the ideas expressed in the second part of this book will re-kindle the interest. In this respect, I was most fortunate in making the acquaintance of Freddie Riley, whose examples of salmon fly tying put the traditional fly right back in its rightful place. And with materials available to all of us! Except in a few instances where stocks have held out, all the materials in his patterns come from birds which are sold only in the food markets of the world, and readily available from the lists of tackle dealers. It is the blending of the colours in the various parts of the fly which has retained the exotic aspect, best seen I think, by comparing the modern illustrations with the original ones in the book. Coupled with the infinite neatness with which the materials are applied, we can now make flies equal in appearance to their ancestors, and for this reason alone, I think readers will understood why I obtained so much satisfaction from being able to present Freddie Riley's methods, and the fine examples of their results.

To illustrate even further, how simple materials can be turned into "exotic" patterns, I was also fortunate in obtaining the assistance of a keen amateur fly-tyer Terry Griffiths, and his patterns, together with coloured photographs, were brought into the book to give further support to my contentions.

He was also responsible, with the help of Ben Johnson – an artist and photographer of international repute – for all the modern photographs in the book. A list of his dressings will be found following on from Freddy Riley's, together with a thumb nail sketch of his background.

I have watched the progress of Terry over several years, and seen the transitional process of his fly-tying range from superb imitations of natural insects, influenced of course by the type of fishing he practised in his native Wales, through the sophistications of modern Reservoir fishing flies, until finally he was drawn naturally to the expressing of his fly-tying as an art form to the field of salmon fly tying.

MAKING SALMON FLIES
FREDDIE RILEY STYLE

Fred Riley showed great promise right from
boyhood as being very talented with his
hands. His father was a brilliant engineer and
gave his son every encouragement in this
direction, and he built his own car whilst in
his early teens. Fred's first adult position
was as a Development Engineer and this was
his employment until he was drafted into the
R.E.M.E. Here, he was trained as a watch-
maker and after cessation of hostilities continued in this field for some time.

He has always shown a great love for
coarse and game fishing, and has won several
trophies in connection with this sport. He
tied his first fly about fifteen years ago, but
his enthusiasm was fired when he watched
George Mortimer of Grantown-on-Spey tie a
"Blue Charm". Then and there he decided

to devote more time to salmon fly tying and during the last year has perfected several new patterns which have created great interest in fly tying circles. His unique method of tying includes the dyeing of his floss silks.

His son Stephen appears to have inherited his father's love of fishing, for he tied his first fly at the age of five years.

BLUE DOCTOR

One of the features Freddie has concentrated on, in fact the main feature, is the extreme neatness and "style" of his flies, and nowhere is this more evident than in the bodies. We will therefore concentrate on this aspect of salmon fly tying, up to the stage where the throat hackle has been tied in and wound, and the fly is already to take its "wings".

The first stage of procedure in all his patterns is the underbody of wool. This is tied in as per Fig. 1, wound to the point where the body will be finished off, and then back again in the manner shown in Fig. 2. It will be observed that each wind is a touching turn, and this is essential if real

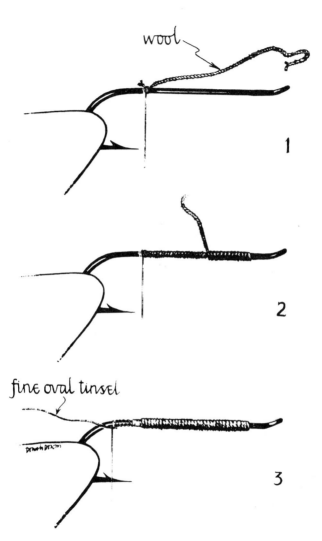

wool

fine oval tinsel

1

2

3

symmetry is to be achieved. The turns of wool are terminated at the position shown in Fig. 3, immediately above the point of the hook, and the tying silk taken to the position also shown in Fig. 3, and fine Oval Tinsel tied in for the Tag.

The winding of the Tag is shown in Figs. 4 & 5, and the object of this method is to have the turns of tinsel wound without having either tying silk or the ends of the tinsel underneath them. This results in a flat tag, with absolutely no distortion.

The silk for the rest of the tag is now tied in and wound as per Fig. 6, ensuring that it tightly covers the two ends of the tinsel.

The tail is tied in at this juncture, as also is the ostrich herl for the butt. I trust that it has not gone unobserved that all this is taking place in the space left at the end of the wool body.

The next step is to wind the butt, and to ensure that the close "ruff" is achieved as in the illustration. This is done by winding to the right, ensuring that the flue is on the left-hand side of its quill not the right. A little experimentation with this part of the

Side view.

4

View from below.

5

Enlarged views of Tag:-

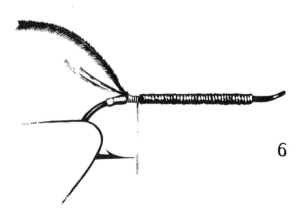

6

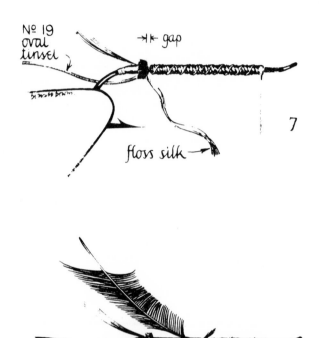

No 19
oval
tinsel

→|←gap

floss silk →

7

8

procedure will soon enlighten you as to the reason for this, if you do not know it already.

Now the Oval tinsel for the rib is tied in followed by the floss silk for the body, and we are still within the space left at the end, Fig. 7. Take the tying silk back to the front of the body, also as shown in this figure, and although this shows the silk as a rib, this is only for clarity of illustration. It actually sinks into the wool underbody.

We now wind turns of the body floss in the remainder of the gap, and when level with the wool underbody we continue to wind the floss up to the stage shown in Fig. 8, where the body hackle is tied in.

It will now be seen that the whole of the rear part of the fly, from the back end of the tag through to the point where the hackle is tied in, is one smooth whole, with no indication where any items were tied in or finished off. This is the whole object of the exercise.

The floss silk is now wound down the rest of the body, continuing the smooth silhouette, followed by turns of the evenly wound tinsel rib, Fig. 9. I would like to mention here, that

9

Freddie prefers to use a Rayon Floss for his bodies to achieve the ultimate in smoothness, and it works. Although narrower than some of the real silks we use, while being wound it tends to spread and lie absolutely flat. Unless one is very careful, real silk can tend to "rope".

Unlike some of us, he ties in his body hackles "undoubled", preferring to "double" them after they are tied in as shown in Fig. 10.

Once the hackle has been "doubled", it is wound to the front of the body, the quill

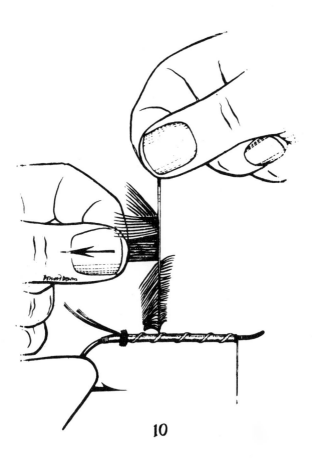

10

being pressed firmly against the oval ribbing tinsel, whilst the hackle fibres are stroked to the rear (Fig. 11). Both these actions ensure that the hackles will have the attractive backward sweep which is the hallmark of a well wound body hackle. Any surplus body hackle is cut off after one complete turn has been made at the front.

The Throat Hackle now has to be tied in and wound (no false hackles here), and this can either be doubled as shown in Fig. 10, or before it is tied in. When this has been completed, firm pressure with the thumb and forefinger is applied as shown in Fig. 12. This ensures that the fibres will be evenly separated, ready for the wings to be added.

PUTTING THE ''ROOF'' ON THE DOCTOR

Basically there is no different between putting on salmon-fly wings and putting on wet trout-fly wings, so anyone who can manage the operation on a trout fly should not be deterred merely because a salmon wing is bigger.

First of all, however, the various strips

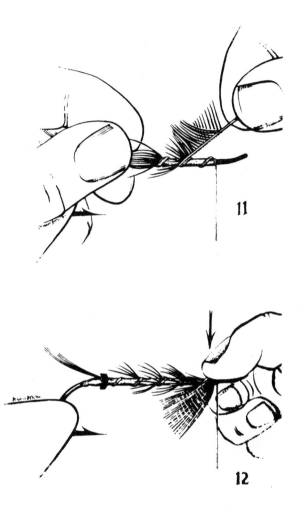

11

12

that go to make the multi-coloured wing must be "married" together, which should present no problem provided one or two simple rules are followed.

Select the necessary feathers and cut sections from each side of each one, laying them on one side until all the slips are ready. One simple rule has to be observed: the slips going into any one of the wings must all come from the same side of the feathers. The best way to ensure this is done is to name the wings "left" and "right", taking all the slips in the "left" wing from the left-hand side of each feather, and all those in the "right" wing from the right-hand side.

You now have to build up the wings by placing the strips edge to edge as shown in Fig. 13. Another simple rule should be followed here in that one should try to have lighter strips at the bottom, finishing up with the darkest at the top. So start with the dyed goose or swan fibres at the bottom, finishing up with darker turkey fibres at the top.

"Marrying" feather-fibres is another technique that looks much harder than it actually is. It is done by placing the bottom strip

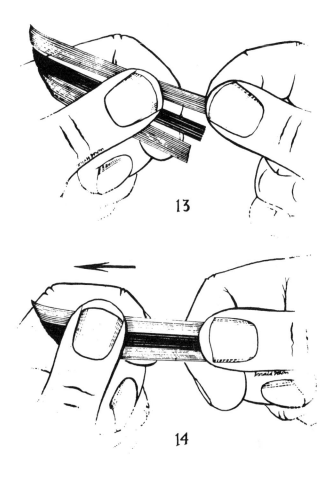

13

14

in the thumb and forefinger of the left hand
(Fig. 13) and laying the next one alongside it,
stroking gently to the left (Fig. 14). You

find that most feathers used in wings lend themselves easily to this process, although one or two, such as golden pheasant-tail fibres and hen pheasant-tail fibres, need a more delicate touch.

A simple but effective method the beginner can use to practise wing "marrying" is to take a fairly wide section from any wing or tail feather, split it longways into several sections, and then join or "marry" them together again.

One little trick you may find useful once all the strips are alongside each other is to hold the wing section by its extremities in the thumbs and forefingers of both hands and then to work them gently in opposite directions. This has the effect of ensuring that all the little hooks which run along the edge of every feather fibre are firmly interlocked.

Treat both wings in this manner, and you are now ready to tie them on to your hook. To ensure that they will lie nice and low over the body, first build up their bed by winding on layers of tying silk until it is level with the front of the body or shoulder of the fly. Failure to do this results in the wing being

pushed firmly up against this shoulder, forc-
ing the wing into an upright position.

Both wing sections are put on at the same
time, tips pointing inwards as for any wet fly,
and with the sweep upwards (Fig.16).There is
a reason for this which I shall explain later.

To further ensure that the wings have a low
profile, use one of two methods. The first
(Fig.15) is called "humping". The wing is held
on top of the hook-shank in the finger and
thumb of the left hand, which also grips the
hook shank very firmly. What will become the
surplus roots of the wings are drawn down by

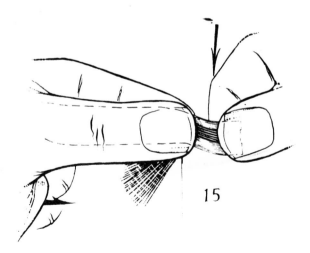

15

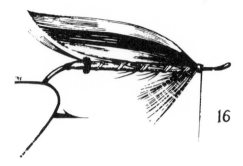

16

the finger and thumb of the right hand, pushing slightly to the left as you do so. This forms the hump you can see just inside the finger and thumb of the left hand. Maintaining the hump, wind the tying silk and hook in the usual manner, using the pinch-and-loop method, drawing the front of the wing firmly down on to its bed. The result should be as in Fig. 16.

The second method used to keep the wing low is the one Freddy Riley uses. Instead of "humping" the fibres he grips the wings very firmly at the point shown in Fig. 15 and then squeezes the protuding fibres down on to the hook-shank with the finger and thumb of the right hand. This, in effect, is what happens to them when the tying silk is pulled tight, but it does ensure that the wing fibres are not being pulled out of alignment during the tying.

You now come to the stage where the "cheeks" and "roof" of the wing are added. In the exotic dressings of earlier times we had a wide variety of feathers to use for cheeks, such as barred summer duck, Lady Amherst pheasant tails, kingfisher feathers, and of course, jungle cock. Fortunately, we can still obtain teal feathers and a strip of these is shown added in Fig.17. These strips, which are each side of the fly, are put in separately, placing each one alongside the wing and tying in with the pinch-and-loop at the wing roots. It is most important that the turns of tying silk are placed only on top of those

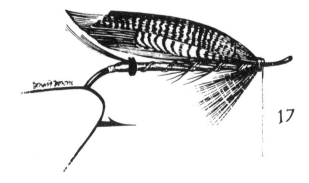

17

already holding the main wings. Any taken to the left will distort the wing, and destroy the symmetry you have tried so hard to attain.

The last stage as far as feather slips are concerned is putting on the brown mallard "roof", and I was very pleased to see that Freddy uses the same method as myself for this purpose. This entails the folding of the strips of brown mallard over the top of the wing instead of placing strips at either side of its top section, and is carried out as follows: cut a left and a right-hand strip from two brown mallard feathers, both double the width required each side of the wing, leaving the quills on. Stroke out the fibres so that they stand at right-angles to the quills. Now place the two strips on top of one another in the same curve, so that their tips are together, leaving a flat double-wing section. Cut off the quills. The flat pieces of feather are then placed on top of the wing, and folded in half so that they envelop the top of it (Fig.17). You will see that the tying silk is still being wound in the same place, and this is how the 'bullet-head' of every well-dressed salmon fly is achieved.

I hope it will now be apparent why the main wing is tied with the tips upswept. By tying in the roof with a downsweep you get a much more cohesive whole than if it swept up in the same way. The two sets of fibres seem to adhere much closer by tying them in this way, and the wing maintains its graceful contours even after it has been well fished.

The final stage of winging is the golden pheasant "topping", which gets its name from the position it has on the fly. These can be tricky feathers to tie on, but one or two tips may help. One is shown in Fig. 18, which illustrates how the main quill can be nicked by the thumb nail. This ensures that

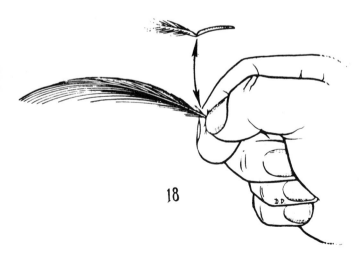

18

when the quill is tied in, the main part of the feathers will slope over the wing as shown in Fig. 19.

Unfortunately, not all toppings come with the correct curve, usually because of the way the feathers have been packed. This can be easily rectified by moistening the feather and laying it on its side on a piece of hardboard and imparting the desired shape to it. When it dries out the imparted shape will remain, and all you need do is brush out the fibres if they are sticking together.

All the "Doctor" flies have red butts and heads, and the former can be wool or ostrich herl (dyed), and the latter wool or red varnish. Fig. 19 shows a piece of wool tied in, and Fig. 20 shows the completed fly after the wool has been wound and the final turns of tying silk added.

As with all fly-tying procedures, practice is most important, and you will find that all the little tips an instructor gives will gradually become incorporated into a natural sequence as your tying improves. One I would like to add here concerns the strips of fibres which go into the married wings. Donald Downs draw-

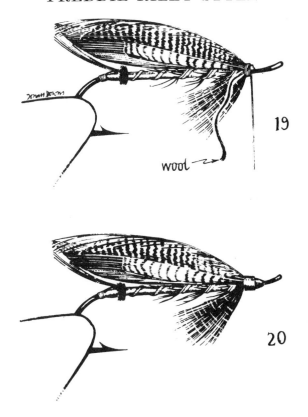

wool

19

20

ings show these in greatly exaggerated form for clarity, whereas in fact they would be much narrower than this. One learns to guage the widths, and, of course, they vary

according to the size of fly being tied and the
number of items in the wing. I generally set
a minimum of three fibres to each slip, as I
find that if one reduces the number to two or
one, the marrying becomes almost impossible
due to the fibres twisting when being stroked.
However, do not make the mistake of using
over-wide strips, as the result is much less
pleasing to the eye.

Substitute feathers. If you have established the
dressings you wish to tie, do not be put off by
the fact that some of the feathers required are
no longer obtainable. One can always find a
reasonable substitute. Here are some.

Red (Indian) Crow. Dyed orange hen hackle
   tips.

Toucan. Dyed light orange or deep yellow hen
   hackle tips, or golden pheasant crests.

Bustard. Speckled turkey tail or wing feather.

Peacock Wing. Mottled turkey wing or tail
   feathers (grey).

Lady Amherst Pheasant Tail. As above.

Blue Chatterer. Blue kingfisher, or if they are
   not available, again dyed hen hackle tips.

Jungle Cock. Many alternatives have been
   devised, some of them very good, thus the

absence of these feathers is not the serious problem it was.

Regretfully I know of no really good substitute for barred summer duck feathers.

PATTERNS

Autumn Gold: (Illustrated)

Tag: Gold tinsel and golden yellow floss.
Tail: A topping and red crow.
Butt: Black ostrich herl.
Body: Two equal sections first flat gold tinsel remainder fiery brown seals fur.
Ribs: Flat copper lurex with silver twist.
Hackle: Red game.
Throat: Guinea fowl.
Wings: Orange, blue, green, yellow and red goose, florican bustard.
Sides: Teal, bronze mallard over, a topping overall.
Head: Black varnish.

Ballater (Illustrated)

Tag: Silver tinsel and golden yellow floss.
Tail: A topping and Indian crow.
Butt: Black herl.
Body: Black floss.
Ribs: Flat gold with oval silver and gold tinsel.
Hackle: A lemon hackle.
Throat: Grey heron.

Wings: A pair of tippets (back to back) veiled with
   married strands of blue, yellow and red goose and
   Amherst pheasant tail.
Sides: Jungle cock, a topping over.
Head: Black varnish.

Blue Magenta

Tag: Silver tinsel and yellow floss.
Tail: A topping.
Butt: Black herl.
Body: Magenta floss.
Ribs: Flat gold and oval silver tinsel.
Hackle: Magenta.
Throat: A pale blue hackle.
Wings: Married strands of yellow, red and blue goose,
   golden pheasant and Amherst pheasant tail, teal,
   strips of brown mallard over.
Sides: Jungle cock, a topping overall.
Head: Black varnish.

Spey Green

Tag: Silver tinsel and golden yellow floss.
Tail: A topping and Indian crow.
Butt: Black herl.
Body: Green lurex.
Ribs: Silver embossed tinsel with oval silver and gold.
Throat: Black heron.
Wings: A pair of tippets (back to back) veiled with
   married strands of red, green, yellow and blue goose.
Sides: Jungle cock, a topping overall.
Head: Black varnish.

Bonny Charles (Illustrated)

Tag: Silver tinsel, dark blue floss.

Tail: A topping.

Butt: Yellow wool.

Body: Two sections first flat gold tinsel remainder purple seals fur.

Ribs: Flat silver tinsel and silver twist.

Hackle: Red game.

Throat: Yellow hackle.

Wings: Red, white, blue and yellow goose, florican bustard.

Sides: Teal, bronze mallard over, a topping overall.

Head: Black varnish.

James Stewart-Fitzroy

Tag: Golden tinsel and magenta floss.

Tail: A topping.

Butt: Yellow wool.

Body: Red lurex.

Ribs: Gold and blue lurex wound side by side.

Throat: A yellow hackle followed by guinea fowl.

Wings: Yellow, orange, red and blue goose, golden pheasant tail and teal, strips of brown mallard over, a topping overall.

Head: Black varnish.

Green Hornet (Illustrated)

Tag: Gold tinsel and orange floss.

Tail: A topping and blue chatterer.

Butt: Yellow wool.

Body: Silver embossed tinsel.

Ribs: Green lurex.

Throat: A lemon hackle followed by guinea fowl.

Wings: Red, yellow and blue goose, florican bustard, golden pheasant tail and teal, strips of brown mallard over, a topping overall.

Head: Black varnish.

Green Sally

Tag: Gold tinsel and magenta floss.

Tail: A topping.

Butt: Black herl.

Body: Green lurex.

Ribs: Oval silver tinsel and black lurex wound side by side.

Hackle: A yellow and green hackle wound together.

Throat: Guinea fowl.

Wings: Married strands of red, green, orange and yellow goose, turkey and golden pheasant tail, teal, strips of brown mallard over.

Sides: Jungle cock, a topping overall.

Head: Black varnish.

Gold'n Blue

Tag: Silver tinsel and yellow floss.

Tail: A topping and blue chatterer.

Butt: Black herl.

Body: Royal blue seals fur.

Ribs: Flat gold and silver oval rinsel.

Hackle: Hot orange.

Throat: Blue guinea fowl.

Wings: Married strands of red, yellow, orange and blue goose, turkey and golden pheasant tail, teal, strips of brown mallard over.

Sides: Jungle cock, a topping overall.

Head: Black varnish.

Red Ranger (Illustrated)

Tag: Flat silver tinsel.

Tail: Topping and blue chatterer.

Butt: Black ostrich herl.

Body: Red floss silk.

Ribs: Flat gold tinsel and silver twist.

Hackle: A lemon hackle.

Throat: Magenta.

Wings: A pair of golden pheasant tippets back to back, veiled with yellow, red and blue goose also florican bustard.

Head: Black varnish.

Silver, Copper 'n Blue

Tag: Silver tinsel and orange floss.

Tail: A topping.

Butt: Red wool.

Body: Blue lurex.

Ribs: Silver embossed tinsel and flat topper lurex.

Throat: Lemon yellow hackle.

Wings: Pair of tippets (back to back) veiled with strands of blue, yellow and red goose and Amherst pheasant tail.

Sides: Jungle cock, a topping over.

Head: Black varnish.

Sir Guest

Tag: Gold tinsel and magenta floss.

Tail: A topping.

Butt: Black herl.

Body: Gold lurex.

Ribs: Oval silver tinsel.

Hackle: Black hackle.

Throat: A lemon hackle.

Wings: A pair of tippets (back to back) veiled with married strands of orange, blue and red goose with florican bustard.

Sides: Jungle cock, a topping over.

Head: Red ostrich herl.

Springtime (Illustrated)

Tag: Gold tinsel, light blue floss.

Tail: Topping and red crow.

Butt: Black ostrich herl.

Body: Three equal sections yellow floss, golden yellow floss, and light green floss.

Ribs: Flat silver tinsel and silver twist.

Hackle: A lemon hackle.

Throat: Light green hackle.

Wings: Married strands of red, blue, yellow, green and orange goose, florican bustard.

Sides: Teal, bronze mallard over, a topping overall.

Head: Black varnish.

Sunrise

Tag: Silver tinsel yellow floss.

Tail: A topping and blue chatterer.

Butt: Purple wool.

Body: Three equal sections of yellow, blue and magenta floss.

Ribs: Flat silver tinsel and gold oval tinsel.

Hackle: Magenta.

Throat: Guinea fowl.

Wings: Red yellow and blue goose, florican bustard, and golden pheasant tail.

Sides: Teal with bronze mallard over, a topping overall.

Head: Black varnish.

Spey Fly: Golden Queen

Body: Flat gold tinsel.
Ribs: Embossed gold tinsel with flat silver tinsel.
Hackle rib: Fine oval silver tinsel.
Hackle: Spey cock hackle or subsittute.
Throat: Light teal or widgeon.
Wings: Bronze mallard strips set short and low.
Head: Black varnish.

Spey Fly: Silver King

Body: Flat silver tinsel.
Ribs: Embossed silver tinsel with flat gold tinsel.
Hackle rib: Fine oval gold tinsel.
Hackle: Spey cock hackle or substitute.
Throat: Light teal or widgeon.
Wings: Bronze mallard strips set short and low.
Head: Black varnish.

TERRY GRIFFITHS & BEN JOHNSON

Terry Griffiths, an amateur fly dresser, was born 1947, and lived in a small village in North Wales, moving away to go to college in the mid-sixties. He learned his fly-fishing the hard way, in North Wales, fishing for 'brownies' on small rivers, taking fish on dry-fly as his preferred style, but for no other reason than it pleased him to fish to rising fish. This was where his fly-dressing began, tying at this stage only out of necessity. There was no help at hand to develop his fly-dressing technically, but plenty of inspiration from angling friends. Many patterns were developed, usually based upon standard dressings, to suit the fishing needs. He dressed his flies by hand, i.e. never having heard of vices, bobbin holders etc., until relatively recently. When these luxuries were employed eventually his flies were, and still are dressed left handed, having learned by holding hooks in his right hand.

Terry Griffiths' fly-dressing developed from small dry flies, to cover the whole range of dressing styles and techniques, when he was exiled to downtown Ealing, with the lack of game fishing facilities in the immediate vicinity he turned to fly dressing as an escape.

Terry Griffiths is an artist by profession, and this is reflected in his attitude towards his fly-dressing, drawing great aesthetic pleasure from dressing salmon flies in particular, but the whole range, trout and salmon is covered by fishing requirements. He is currently researching and following the development of fly dressing in the United States and Canada.

Ben Johnson the photographer was born 1946, an artist living and working in London. He has exhibited in New York and London, presently exhibiting with Fischer Fine Art, London. The collaboration with Terry Griffiths grew out of a sympathy for the formal disciplines of each others work – Terry Griffiths' fly dressing – Ben Johnsons' painting.

PATTERNS

Adjutant (Illustrated)

Tag: Fine oval silver; golden yellow floss
Tail: Topping
Butt: Black ostrich herl.
Body: Black floss
Rib: Silver lace, flat silver
Hackle: Black cock hackle
Throat: Orange cock hackle.
Wing: Tippet in strands; peacock, yellow, orange, red goose 'married'; teal sides, mallard over; topping over all.
Sides: Jungle cock
Cheeks: Blue kingfisher
Head: Black varnish

Black Joke (Illustrated)

Tag: Fine flat silver
Tail: Topping
Butt: Black ostrich herl.
Body: Black floss
Rib: Silver lace, orange floss, oval silver
Hackle: Black cock

Throat: Bodyhackle carried forward

Wing: Tippet; peacock, amherst, yellow, red goose, 'married'. Bronze mallard over. Topping over all.

Sides: Jungle cock

Head: Black varnish

Blue Joke (Illustrated)

Tag: Fine flat silver

Tail: Topping

Butt: Black ostrich herl.

Body: Blue floss

Rib: Oval silver; golden floss, flat silver.

Hackle: Grey heron

Throat: Light blue cock hackle.

Wing: Tippet; green, orange, blue goose 'married'; brown mallard over; topping over all.

Sides: Jungle cock

Head: Black varnish

Candlelight (Illustrated)

Tag: Fine round silver thread, lemon yellow floss

Tail: Topping

Butt: Black ostrich herl.

Body: In three equal parts: white D.F.M. wool, lemon yellow seal fur, amber seal fur.

Rib: Silver lace, flat silver

Hackle: Lemon yellow

Throat: Scarlet

Wing: Tippet; white, red, yellow, red goose; bronze (brown) mallard over, topping over all.

Sides: Jungle cock

Head: Black varnish

Embers (Illustrated)

Tag: Flat silver
Tail: Topping
Butt: Black ostrich herl.
Body: Claret floss
Rib: Silver lace, orange floss, flat silver
Hackle: Claret
Throat: Teal Flank.
Wing: Tippet, red, orange, yellow goose; brown mallard over; topping over all.
Sides: Jungle cock
Head: Black varnish

Wrack (Illustrated)

Tag: Fine flat silver
Tail: Topping
Butt: Black ostrich herl.
Body: Medium blue floss
Rib: Silver lace, flat silver
Hackle: Dark blue
Throat: Light green (Highlander)
Wing: Peacock sword, topping over
Sides: Jungle cock
Cheek: Red goose (Ibis substitute)
Head: Black varnish